179

Mormon Songs from the Rocky Mountains

A Compilation of Mormon Folksong

Publications of the American Folklore Society
Memoir Series
General Editor, John Greenway
Volume 53   ·   1968

MORMON SONGS

From the Rocky Mountains

A Compilation of Mormon Folksong

Edited by
THOMAS E. CHENEY

PUBLISHED FOR THE AMERICAN FOLKLORE SOCIETY BY
THE UNIVERSITY OF TEXAS PRESS • AUSTIN & LONDON

Library of Congress Catalog Card No. 68–63018
Copyright © 1968 by the American Folklore Society
All rights reserved

Printed by the University of Texas Printing Division, Austin
Bound by Universal Bookbindery, Inc., San Antonio

To My Wife, Fern

Who despite my neglect continues to be more devoted to me than I am to my folklore obsession. She has gone with me on field trips and waited interminably while I recorded songs and stories and has done it both patiently and impatiently. She has helped me in research, edited my work, and sacrificed social pleasures. All of this she has done pleasantly, efficiently, and reluctantly.

ACKNOWLEDGMENTS

The work of collecting, recording, selecting, and editing materials for this publication was made possible through the help of the Research Department of Brigham Young University.

In music transcription from tapes to copy I was ably assisted by my daughter Karla Dawn Taylor.

Dr. Austin Fife and his wife Alta, folklorists of Utah State University and well known authorities in this field, have graciously allowed me to use some of their materials. Olive Woolley Burt, a writer of renown and a folklorist of good repute, also contributed freely from her large collection. This book is the work of many people—authors of individual songs, singers who have preserved them, and contributors who gave them to this collection. Most of the authors are unknown folk, long since gone. And of all things, I want least to offend the dead. To them, the known and the unknown authors of these songs, I give my thanks.

PREFACE

The songs in this book are not exclusively the findings of one collector. In order to make the work more definitive I have used, by permission, certain valuable songs from the collections of Austin and Alta Fife, Olive W. Burt, and others.

Austin and Alta Fife, who were among the first to plow the ground extensively in this field, have the following to say about the wealth of Mormon folksong:

So abundant are the songs that the Mormon folk have composed and sung at all of the critical moments in their history that, were every other document destroyed, it would still be possible, from the folk songs alone, to reconstruct in some detail the story of their theology, their migrations, their conflict with the Gentiles, and the founding and development of most of their settlements from New York to San Bernardino.[1]

This statement may seem extravagant, yet it becomes credible as one learns more about Mormon folksong.

The songs I have collected from Mormons were not all composed by them or about them; they include songs the Mormon folk sang. They were collected for the historical and social values they reveal —such as how people lived, what they did, what they thought, and what they loved—and for their literary and musical values. However, for this publication, only songs that have a specific Mormon relationship by composition or subject matter are used. My collection now contains more than a thousand songs; some of the first were included in a Master's thesis completed at the University of Idaho in 1936. I have twenty hours of tape recordings from the contributors. Most of these singers if still alive are people over seventy, survivors of a former folksinging society. The music of most of the songs herein is transcribed from versions recorded on these tapes. Austin Fife's collection of about twenty recorded hours

[1] Austin E. Fife and Alta Fife, *Saints of Sage and Saddle*, p. 316.

of songs and stories has been examined and some of its specifically Mormon songs are used.

In collecting I have held rigidly to the rule of accepting songs only from oral tradition or from manuscript journals preserved by the families of the early folksingers. Absolute status of a song in relation to the folk, however, is often impossible to determine.

Mormons wrote songs. It is a common experience for a collector to meet someone who says, "Here is a song which my grandfather wrote when . . ." Whenever possible I have tried to identify the composer and to obtain original words and music from the composer's relatives or descendants. Words and music given here may coincide with other published versions. The texts copied from manuscripts or journals of the composers are often identical with texts which I have collected from other singers. However, when research identified a certain composer and produced the original, I have used the original.

Songs dealing with Mormon history are folksongs, not through oral circulation for generations, but rather through having been composed by folk, who often paraphrase other songs. They write pertinently about the folk, catching the spirit of the group so effectively that the community accepts the composition as its own. This is the modern folk process in Mormondom, the inevitable method of circulation in a literate society in which everything is written. These are no less the property of the folk than are minstrel ballads such as "Chevy Chase" in which literary quality is too prominently evident to suggest wide oral circulation.

The songs appearing in this book are classified according to types—songs treating Mormon history or subject matter, Mormon locale, Mormon customs and teachings, and satire and criticism of Mormons.

In popularizing Mormon folksong, credit must be given to singers as well as collectors. Recently Rosalie Sorrels commercially recorded nineteen Mormon pioneer songs, fifteen of which are in this collection in the same or in different versions.[2] Earlier, the Library of Congress had cut a record of some of these songs from the Fife collection.[3]

[2] Rosalie Sorrels, *Songs of the Mormon Pioneers*, edited by Austin E. Fife for the Columbia Research Group.

[3] Duncan Emrich, *Songs of the Mormons and Songs of the West*, Library of Congress, AAFS L30.

In 1965 a Legacy Record of Mormon folksong treating the trek west and the settlement in the intermountain country was produced by Columbia Records with accompanying written and pictorial account; I was folklore adviser for this work, and all of its songs are included here.[4]

To the folksingers themselves must be given credit for most of this work. Some deserve particular attention. Eliza Jane Avery, of Burley, Idaho, and her son William H. Avery, both now deceased, gave freely and generously. Mrs. Avery was a Mormon pioneer to the mountain country who lived and reared her family in Huntington, Utah. Throughout her lifetime she learned songs and taught them to her children. At the time that I met her she was about eighty years old but she had a good memory for old songs, which she had never copied. Her son William retained some twenty songs in his memory, none of which he had ever seen written.

Huntington, Utah, was also the locale of the singing Wakefields. Don Wakefield, now deceased, knew over two hundred songs which he learned from his parents and from people he met while he worked around the country as a sheep shearer, cowboy, farm hand, and railroader. His brother M. E. Wakefield of Ogden, Utah, is over ninety years old, still in fair voice, and plays the same banjo to accompany himself that he played in his twenties. He has written down his complete repertory of over four hundred songs. Though some of these songs cannot be called folksongs, the collection contains many excellent ballads and lyrics of value to the folksong collector.

A very excellent, energetic singer and collector of songs dealing with Mormon history and Mormon subject matter is Lolovi McMurrin Hilton of Ogden, Utah. Mr. Hilton uses his excellent voice willingly whenever asked. Now seventy years old, he has for over thirty years worked as a law enforcement officer in Ogden. A loyal Mormon, he comes from pioneer stock in both the Hilton and McMurrin lines. His parents, before his birth, had served as missionaries in Samoa (where they got the name Lolovi). Early in the boy's life the family moved into a Mormon community in Mexico which was right for folksinging.

Mr. Hilton's interest in the Church has led him to give special attention to preserving songs of Mormon subject matter. He says:

---

[4] Goddard Lieberson, *The Mormon Pioneers,* Thomas E. Cheney, consultant, Columbia Records, LL1023.

It was in 1946 when everybody was preparing for the big Centennial Year in 1947 that I was visited by Austin Fife who was gathering folklore. This was really the first time that I realized that I had learned a lot of old songs in my boyhood. I sang more than twenty songs for Dr. Fife and his wife for the Library of Congress. I soon became known as a Utah folksong singer and I filled one hundred forty engagements in Utah and Idaho during the Centennial Year.

Dr. Willard Rhodes of Columbia University collected thirty-one songs from Mr. Hilton in 1952. Since 1952 Mr. Hilton's repertory has grown: on my tapes is recorded his complete collection of seventy-eight songs.

A sizable block of songs was contributed to this collection by Pat Matheny, who obtained the songs from the Harvey Taylor family of the Mormon colony in Mexico.

Mrs. Lang of Milford, Utah, and her brother Jesse Jepsen of St. George, Utah, were folksong preservers discovered by Robert Christmas. Their father, James Jepsen, long since dead, left the legacy of a manuscript of his songs to his daughter and a voice to sing them to his son. Jesse sang beautifully at seventy-four, both songs his father taught him and songs he obtained elsewhere. From this couple came many songs. Some of these choice songs are published herein.

Mr. and Mrs. Karl Larson of St. George, Utah, gave valuable assistance and materials to this work. Mr. Larson gave songs he had gathered from the St. George area, some of which were published in his history of the town of Washington, Utah, *The Red Hills of November*; and Mrs. Larson contributed songs from a manuscript inherited from her grandfather, Charles L. Walker, who, with others, was sent to St. George by Brigham Young to colonize the country. Being somewhat of a creative artist, he composed songs and poems for many occasions; many of these were sung for years, not only in Utah's Dixie, but elsewhere in the Church. Zaidee Walker Miles, mother of Mrs. Larson, wrote in a "Life Story" of her father, Charles L. Walker, the following:

He wrote something for nearly every celebration of the 24th of July up to the time of his death. His poems, "humble and homely" though they be, contain much of the history of early life in the valley. They paint a more vivid picture of conditions during the early days than will ever be found between the covers of history books.

Through the work of Jay Healy came Mrs. Jenny Hancock's

contribution to this work. Reared in a Mormon settlement in Colorado near the southern border of Utah, Mrs. Hancock learned and sang songs to entertain young people in that sparsely populated area. When asked to record songs on my tapes, she willingly complied, thereby providing me with many excellent melodies. Among her notebook songs are some of the compositions of Levi Hancock, the Mormon Battalion song writer and an ancestor of Mrs. Hancock's husband.

Lenn Shumway permitted me to use his valuable collection of songs from Taylor, Arizona.

Another contributor of a significant group of songs is S. A. Harris, now deceased, of American Fork, Utah. Many of the thirty-three songs in Mr. Harris' manuscript are traditional ballads which often are touched with a delightful modern influence.

Many other people have contributed significant additions to the total collection and to this book. The names of these contributors appear with the songs.

Since this study is not a comparative study of American folksong, a listing of all other sources where the songs can be found is of little value. However, in order to give those collectors credit who have done significant work in collecting and publishing Mormon folksong, I have listed those sources, and for the few songs appearing here which have been given a number in G. Malcolm Laws, Jr., *Native American Balladry*, I have given the number.

If the source from which I obtained the words of a song was a singer whose recording is on my tapes, I have listed it as "sung by . . ." with the name of the singer, place, and date following. In every case where a singer is listed I have used the music contributed by that singer. If I was able to find the original text from a diary, journal, publication, manuscript, or copy made by the author, I have used the original and indicated the source.

CONTENTS

Acknowledgments. ix
Preface xi

I. Introduction to Mormon Folksong 3

II. Songs Dealing With Mormon History 23
   1. The Story of Mormonism   *M* 26
   2. Tittery-Irie-Aye   *M* 31
   3. Campaign for General Smith 33
   4. Mormon Battalion Song   *M* 35
   5. All Hail the Brave Battalion 40
   6. The Desert Route 41
   7. The Bullfight on the San Pedro   *M* 42
   8. The Lonesome Roving Wolves 46
   9. The Mormon Battalion Song 47
  10. The Camp of Israel 49
  11. Whoa, Haw, Buck and Jerry Boy   *M* 50
  12. The Ox Team Trail   *M* 51
  13. The Way We Crossed the Plains   *M* 54
  14. Ye Elders of Israel   *M* 55
  15. California 57
  16. Our Ain Mountain Hame 59
  17. Zion, the Home of an Honest Man 61
  18. The Bull Whacker   *M* 61
  19. The Handcart Song   *M* 64
  20. The Handcart Song (Missionary) 66
  21. The Upper California   *M* 68
  22. This Is the Place (or)
     Brigham Young, the Western Pioneer   *M* . . . 69
  23. This Is the Place 72
  24. Sego Lily   *M* 73
  25. The Campfire Meeting (or)
     Gather Round the Campfire, Brethren   *M* . . . 75
  26. The Seagulls and the Crickets   *M* 76
  27. Is the Story True?   *M* 78
  28. In Defense of Polygamy   *M* 80
  29. Put You Into Limbo 82
  30. Ever Constant 83
  31. Doo Dah   *M* 84

32. If Uncle Sam's Determined 86
33. Johnston's Army Episode 87
34. Strong Is the Power of Brigham's God 89
35. The United Order   M 90
36. Brighter Days in Store (or)
    Brigham's Hard Times Come Again No More . . 91
37. The Utah Iron Horse   M 92
38. Echo Canyon   M 94
39. The Railroad Cars, They're Coming 96
40. The Iron Horse 97
41. Bless Brigham Young   M 98
42. Brigham Young's Birthday 99
43. The Dying Prophet 99
44. The Mormon Tabernacle   M 101
45. The Gospel News Is Sounding 103
46. Pioneer Day 1870   M 105
47. All Are Talking of Utah 108
48. Conference Time 110
49. Passing Through   M 111

III. Songs of Mormon Country Locale 113
    50. St. George and the Drag-on   M 113
    51. Marching to Dixie 116
    52. St. George and Mormon Dixie 117
    53. Once I Lived in Cottonwood   M 118
    54. The Drunkards of Bonanza 120
    55. Lo A Temple   M 123
    56. Pounding Rock Into the Temple Foundation . . 125
    57. Song For the Temple Volunteers 126
    58. Logan Temple   M 126
    59. We the Boys of Sanpete County 128
    60. Down in Utah   M 130
    61. My House   M 132
    62. Pleasant Valley   M 133
    63. Blue Mountain   M 135
    64. Oh Timpanogas, Mighty Timpanogas   M . . . 137
    65. Teton Peaks   M 138

IV. Mormon Customs and Teachings 141
    66. None Can Preach the Gospel Like the
        Mormons Do   M 142

67. A Church Without a Prophet 144
68. Carrot Greens 145
69. Oh Touch Not the Wine Cup   M 146
70. Have Courage, My Boy, To Say No!   M 148
71. Be Home Early Tonight, My Dear Boy   M . . . 150
72. The Good Old Keg of Wine 152
73. Ditches Break Again No More 153
74. A Burlesque on the Fashions of the Day, 1870
       (or) The Grecian Bend   M 154
75. Sparking Sunday Night   M 156
76. Julius Hannig's Wedding   M 158
77. Charlie Knell's Wedding   M 160
78. The Loafer's Lament 161
79. Waste Not, Want Not   M 162
80. Cold Winter Is Coming   M 164
81. Mogos, Nogos, Everybody Come   M 167
82. The Mormon Sunday School Song 168
83. Thirty Pieces of Silver 169
84. Mottos on the Wall   M 170
85. The Lifeboat   M 172

V. Satire and Sin 174
86. Brigham, Brigham Young   M 176
87. Zack, the Mormon Engineer   M 179
88. A Marriage Proposal 182
89. The Mormon Coon 183
90. Sweet Betsy from Pike 184
91. The Good Old Yankee Doodle 185
92. Don't Marry the Mormon Boys   M 186
93. The Merry Mormons 187
94. Christine LeRoy   M 189
95. Porter Rockwell 191
97. Wheat 192
97. The Kanab Tragedy 193
98. The Orderville Murder 195
99. The Double Tragedy 197
100. Mountain Meadows Massacre   M 200

Bibliography 207
Index of Song Titles and First Lines 211
Index 216

Mormon Songs from the Rocky Mountains

A Compilation of Mormon Folksong

CHAPTER I

Introduction to Mormon Folksong

On the 26th of July, 1847, the second day after the arrival of the pioneer company of Mormons in Salt Lake Valley, a group of men climbed to the top of a hill north of the present Salt Lake City and named it Ensign Peak. Later, on this peak a "liberty pole" was raised from which floated the Stars and Stripes.

The ensign the Latter-day Saints pioneers had in mind and of which they had frequently spoken en route west was meant to represent all nations as a sign and ensign of the "Empire of Christ." J. W. Gunnison, who spent the winter of 1849–1850 in Salt Lake Valley, refers to the prevalent idea among the settlers at that time:

> To the north of temple block, and close by, towers up and overlooks the temple city, the Ensign Mound. It terminates the great spur, and is conspicuous in approaching the city, from every quarter. On this mountain peak there is soon to be unfurled the most significant flag ever thrown to the breeze, constructed out of the banners of all peoples. Joined in symbolical unity, "the flag of all nations" shall wave above the sacred temple; and then shall they verify the decree given by the Prophet Isaiah: "All ye inhabitants of the world, and dwellers on the earth, see ye, when he lifteth up an Ensign on the mountains" [Isaiah XVIII:3] ... "And he will lift up an Ensign to the nations from afar, and will hiss unto them from the end of the earth; and, behold, they shall come with speed swiftly" [Isaiah V:26].
> ... "And it shall come to pass in the last days, that the mountain of the Lord's house shall be established in the top of the mountains, and shall be exalted above the hills; and all nations shall flow unto it."
> [Isaiah II:2][1]

Some years later Parley P. Pratt wrote a hymn called "Zion's Standard," the words of which express pioneer thinking:

[1] B. H. Roberts, *A Comprehensive History of the Church of Jesus Christ of Latter-day Saints*, III, 277.

> Lo! the Gentile chain is broken,
>   Freedom's banner waves on high;
> List, ye nations! by this token,
>   Know that your redemption's nigh.
>
> See, on yonder distant mountain,
>   Zion's standard wide unfurled,
> Far above Missouri's fountain,
>   *Lo, it waves for all the world.*
>
> Freedom, peace and full salvation
>   Are the blessings guaranteed,
> Liberty to every nation,
>   Every tongue, and every creed.
>
> Come, ye Christian sects, and pagan,
>   Pope, and Protestant, and Priest,
> Worshipers of God or Dragon,
>   Come ye to fair freedom's feast.
>
> Come, ye sons of doubt and wonder,
>   Indian, Moslem, Greek or Jew,
> All your shackles burst asunder,
>   Freedom's banner waves for you.[2]

Since the day when the Mormon Prophet Joseph Smith turned his eyes toward the Rocky Mountains, the Mormons have been obsessed with love for Zion, destined by prophecy to be exalted above the hills. The granite mountains have symbolized the Rock of Ages. The Mormons felt that they were victims of persecution. They believed that they were mistreated in New York, maligned in Ohio, maliciously persecuted and driven from Missouri, and forced to flee from Illinois because of the viciousness of mobs who had murdered their leader. Thus they were forced to flee to the mountains.

Before reaching their chosen refuge they sang, "Lift up thine eyes to the mountains whence cometh thy strength."

> Behold the mountain of the Lord
> In latter days shall rise
> On mountain tops above the hills
> And draw the wondering eyes.[3]

With a fervor that became a passion they loved and to this day

[2] Roberts, *Ibid.*, 277.
[3] *Hymns, Church of Jesus Christ of Latter-day Saints* (Salt Lake City, 1948) 297.

continue to love their mountain home. Note the strength of symbol and depth of devotion expressed in various Mormon hymns:

High on a mountain top a banner is unfurled,
Ye nations, now look up, it waves to all the world. . . .
On Zion's mount behold it stands.[4]

Zion stands with hills surrounded,
Zion kept by power divine . . .
Happy Zion, what a favored lot is thine![5]

For the strength of the hills, we bless thee,
Our God, our father's God;
Thou hast made thy children mighty
By the touch of the mountain sod. [6]

Mountains capped with virgin snow,
Utah, star of the West.[7]

Land of the mountains high,
Utah, we love thee.[8]

Holy temples on Mount Zion
In lofty splendor shine.[9]

Our mountain home so dear, where crystal waters clear
Flow ever free . . .
In sylvan depth and shade, in forest and in glade,
Where'er we pass,
The hand of God we see in leaf and bud and tree
Or bird or humming bee or blade of grass.[10]

Let the mountains shout for joy,
Let the valleys ring . . .
Let them all burst forth into song . . .
For the wilderness has blossomed,
Blossomed like the rose,
And the barren desert is a fruitful field.
Joy and gladness now are found therein,
Thanksgiving and the voice of melody.[11]

---

[4] *Ibid.*, p. 62.
[5] *Ibid.*, p. 212.
[6] *Ibid.*, p. 241.
[7] *Ibid.*, p. 72.
[8] *Ibid.*, p. 140.
[9] *Ibid.*, p. 63.
[10] *Ibid.*, p. 144.
[11] Evan Stephens, Behuin Choral Series, No. 1119, Mormon Tabernacle Choir Sheet Music.

The songs in this collection are the expression of the Mormon people and here, too, are many references to mountains, such as:

> We will build our homes in safety
> Where the mountain bulwark stands;
> We can serve our Lord and here be happy
> In this sacred, promised land.[12]

> To California's land we'll go,
> Where from the mountain wine doth flow;
> A land of peace and liberty,
> To California, go with me. . . .
> For on the Mount our king shall reign.[13]

> For there the prophets have declared
> The house of God shall be,
> On mountain tops it shall be reared
> That all the world may see.[14]

> And in that New Jerusalem the righteous will be found . . .
> In Zion's city there we'll build a temple to our Lord.[15]

> Soon Zion in her beauty will shine forth upon the world,
> In glorious light and majesty when freedom's flag's
>   unfurled,
> And kings and queens from far, who hear of her fame,
> Will come to see her glory in our ain mountain hame.[16]

In a more secular vein,

> Blue Mountain with horsehead on your side,
> You have won my love to keep.[17]

> Timpanogas, mighty Timpanogas,
> Timpanogas, mountain that I love,[18]

> To the east are the Teton Peaks
> Stealing my heart from me.[19]

These, then, are the songs of a mountain-loving people—they did not come singing *out* of the wilderness many long years ago; they came singing *into* the wilderness of Utah many long years ago.

---

[12] In "Gather Round the Campfire," Song No. 25.
[13] In "California," Song No. 15.
[14] In "Zion, the Home of an Honest Man," Song No. 17.
[15] In "The Gospel News Is Sounding," Song No. 45.
[16] In "Our Ain Mountain Hame," Song No. 16.
[17] In "Blue Mountain," Song No. 63.
[18] In "Timpanogas, Mighty Timpanogas," Song No. 64.
[19] In "Teton Peaks," Song No. 65.

Hardships, poverty, and limited means of entertainment were mothers of invention which led to widespread folk creativity. The songs in this collection reveal the manners and mores, the aims and ambitions, likes and dislikes, loves and hates of the society that produced and preserved them. To me it reveals a people who are sentimental, highly emotional, kind, sincere, friendly, devoted to loved ones, loyal to their leaders, intolerant of outsiders, self-satisfied, proud of their own brand of righteousness, and able to laugh at themselves and others.

To justify my generalization about Mormon character, I include here a brief examination of Mormon beliefs and attitudes. From the time the Church was organized in 1830 until the present day, the society has been taught and has held to the notion that the Lord's people are not to be people of the world. If they have chosen God and God has chosen them, then they must live as God would have them live. They interpret every phase of life in terms of religion. Believing firmly that man is not exalted by grace of God alone, but rather through continued effort of the individual in living the good life, they attempt to order their lives accordingly. Individuals differ in this society as in others in their beliefs, interpretations, and behavior. Yet in the main the Mormons feel secure in their faith, in the belief that it provides the pattern which will enable followers to get the most out of this life and the best rewards in the life to come.

The folksongs composed by the Mormons about Mormon history reveal a belief in and support of the Church, its doctrine, its teaching, its inspired leadership, and its divine origin. Devotion to the Church is sometimes carried to the point of being kin to the vice of pride.

The feeling of certainty, of knowing exactly who is on the Lord's side, leads also to a spirit which might not always be interpreted as that of Christlike forgiveness, but rather as a spirit of "love your friends and hate your enemies." In the song "In Defense of Polygamy" officials sent to Utah to enforce the law designed to stamp out polygamy are condemned:

> Old Ireland and his aids will go below,
> And Dixon will do well to engage a case in Hell,
> For the road he's on will take him there I know.

From the time the Church was established in New York to the

present day, loyalty to the Church and to Church leaders usually has been placed above loyalty to the government when the two were found to be in conflict. When Johnston's Army was sent to Utah, the motives of government officials were strongly questioned, and Brigham Young prepared to protect his empire. Attitude of the folk toward his action is expressed in song:

> Then let us be on hand
> By Bringham Young to stand
> And if our enemies do appear
> We'll sweep them from the land.

The Mormon people believe in divine revelation, not only that coming through holy men of old and recorded in biblical canon, but also that coming through holy men of modern days. They believe that God did not seal the heavens in the distant past and leave the world without prophets in this era. Joseph Smith and subsequent presidents of the Church are prophets, seers, and revelators. The folk accept and believe that God reveals His will to people of this day through His modern prophets. Thus loyalty to Joseph Smith and Brigham Young is evident among the folksinging group.

This loyalty, however, does not completely blind them to the reality of everyday, mundane problems. The trek across the plains from Nauvoo, Illinois, to Salt Lake Valley, the struggle with opposing elements of nature in their desert home, the fight for survival, the colonizing of outlying, barren areas in the intermountain country where drought and indifferent nature opposed them, the building of houses of worship under adverse conditions—all these, recorded in song, reveal an awareness of the common tendency among men to examine the motives of the leadership and at times to oppose authority. Yet this opposition is usually condemned. In "Marching To Dixie" these lines appear:

> There's a certain man in Dixie whose faith began to fail,
> He measured Mormon Dixie by the breadth of his thumb nail,
> Now when he gets converted, he will tell a different tale.

More critical of leadership is a stanza from "Once I Lived in Cottonwood":

> I feel so weak and hungry now, there's nothing here to cheer
> Except prophetic sermons, which we very often hear.
> They will hand them out by dozens and prove them by
>   the book—
> I'd rather have some roasting ears to stay at home and cook.

I feel so weak and hungry now, I think I'm nearly dead;
'Tis seven weeks last Sunday since I have tasted bread.

There are also anti-Mormon songs circulated by these "saints of
sage and saddle." Mormons, like their "Gentile" neighbors, recognize sin, sometimes even within the "holy of holies."

The tone more prominently in evidence in this collection, however, is that of unquestioned loyalty, as in the following lines:

> Brigham Young, the western pioneer,
> Brigham Young won a noble race.

and

> "This is the place," the speaker said,
> "Where Brigham Young himself was led
> By God's hand . . .

Since the Mormon Church is founded on the concept of continued
revelation from God, and members of the Church believe in the
possibility of certain people being spokesmen for God, a highly
idealized conception of life has been portrayed in their song. With
God as the leader of His people and the Prophet as His spokesman,
whatever occurred was God's will. Whether life's great questions
were answered or unanswered, whatever existed was right. If man
could not see God's purpose, the reason was man's limited eyesight.
A typical reaction toward good fortune and misfortune is evident in
the behavior patterns of the men in the Mormon Battalion. They
interpreted their misfortunes as punishment permitted by a benevolent God to bring them nearer to Him, and their valor in meeting
misfortune nobly as pleasing to Him. In their great migration west,
pioneers were continuously buoyed up in spirit by an assurance of
God's leadership; if God led the Israelites to the Promised Land,
would He not lead them? Mormons, like the Israelites, felt that God
was with them by day and night, and, though hardship, disease,
and disaster came, they felt that "if they lived, they lived unto the
Lord; and if they died, they died unto the Lord." No matter what
occurred, they continued to sing "All is well."

Though they suffered, they looked for a better day. In "The Ox
Team Trail" appear the words:

> Bound for a realm of peace
> Where strife among the world,
> The world and them might cease.

As certain migrating groups pushed handcarts full of possessions from Iowa to Salt Lake Valley over rocky roads and mountain passes, they sang:

> When you get there among the rest,
> Obedient be and you'll be blessed
> And in God's chambers be shut in
> While judgments cleanse the world from sin.

And to the end they rejoiced:

> . . . thank the day we made a start
> To cross the plains in our handcart.

God is recognized as the benevolent father in His saving the pioneers from starvation when crickets were destroying the grain crops. In the song "The Seagulls and the Crickets," the story is told of the utter horror experienced by the people when crickets came in hordes to destroy the crops:

> And the finger of devastation marked
> Its course on the Mormon host.
> With a vigor that desperation fanned
> They battled and smote and slew,
> But the clouds still gathered and broke afresh
> Till the fields that waved were few.
>
> With visions of famine and want and woe
> They prayed from hearts sincere
> When lo, from the west came other clouds
> To succor the pioneers.

The songs presented in this book might give the impression that Mormons have not been part of the great folksinging masses of America. In all Mormon collections—by the Fifes, Hubbard, Davidson, Burt, Shumway, and others—are songs brought to the West from other areas. In these collections, as well as in my own extensive collection, are songs that give evidence that Mormon people were very much a part of the world. They soaked up life from being in it; they were part of the great melée in the settlement of the West. They sang cowboy and Indian and railroad and outlaw and even hillbilly songs because these were part of the great West. They loved their children like other parents and sang to them the songs that other parents sang. They were sentimental as other people were sentimental and cried over things worth crying over and over things not worth a tear. They would clown and play and laugh and sing the joyful songs for all the reasons others do—all these things they did because they were part of mankind.

At the time the Mormons came West there were hundreds of others—"Gentiles"—on the trails. The Mormon pioneers were only a part of the great mass of people who conquered the West. Steinbeck in his short story "The Leader of the People" has the grandfather who lived in the past express his feeling for the movement:

It wasn't Indians that were important, nor adventures, nor even getting out here. It was a whole bunch of people made into one big crawling beast. It was westering and westering. Every man wanted something for himself, but the big beast that was all of them wanted only westering. . . . When we saw the mountains at last we cried—all of us. But it wasn't getting here that mattered, it was movement and westering. . . . The westering was as big as God, and the slow steps that made the movement piled up and piled up until the continent was crossed.

Because the Mormons were a part of this big, masculine movement, they sang songs about the West; if they sang more strongly and more frequently, it was because their Church gave them a uniqueness of spirit and cohesion.

All the Indian songs in my collection show significant white man-Indian relationships. The first type, including "The Sioux Indians," "Valley of Custer," "The Texas Ranger," and "Haunted Falls," show the violence and savagery of Indian warfare. The second type, "Bright Amanda," "Fallen Leaf," "The Lass of Mohea," and "White Man, Let Me Go," show brotherly love and friendly interchange between the two societies. Brigham Young's philosophy, "It is cheaper to feed the Indians than to fight them," and the prevalent efforts of Mormons to maintain friendly relations (as demonstrated in the work of such leaders as Jacob Hamblin) are reflected in songs of mutual understanding. These songs, however, may have appeared as a result of guilt feelings on the part of white men for having mistreated the Indians and may therefore be belated attempts to make restitution. One thing is evident; they appealed to the folk idealism of the Mormons.

Cattle raising was a major occupation among Mormons. Austin and Alta Fife fittingly named their book about them *Saints of Sage and Saddle*. The Wasatch and Teton Mountain Country has its cowboys, its vigorous westerners: not the pseudo-cowboys of Hollywood and television westerns, but the true cattlemen who know cows better than they do guitars, and branding irons better than

shooting irons. Many songs of my collection came from the repertory of W. Ezra Allred of Paris, Idaho, who owned large herds of
Hereford cattle which he ranged on state land and fed in the marsh
country at the north end of Bear Lake. I have ridden horses with
Ezra Allred, he riding his favorite horse, Tex, an alert bay that appeared to know naturally how to turn a cow. Ezra Allred was not a
singer who entertained crowds, yet he knew the cowboy songs and
sang them as he rode the range on mountain trails. He sang "The
Cowboy's Lament" (which he called "The Dying Cowboy") to a
different tune from any I have heard elsewhere. He knew "Red
River Valley," "The Strawberry Roan," and "When the Work's All
Done This Fall."

Mr. Allred died before I began collecting, but his family, working
together, remembered many of his songs. This cattleman was typical of many Mormon men. Cattlemen and sheep men riding the
wide open ranges sang to pass the hours and to amuse themselves,
learning songs from each other. Of these men who knew horses
better than motors and who sang songs they learned from other cowboys, only a remnant remains—but the account is not completely
closed. Other range riders, vigorous westerners who communicated
their love of nature through folksong lyrics and who contributed to
this collection, were W. H. Avery and Don Wakefield.

From Don Wakefield I collected the delightful "Zebra Dun";
from Lenn Shumway an old version of "Home on the Range" with
different music; from John Bircher, "Utah Carrol"; and from various other singers, other cowboy songs.

Effective wheels of progress came to the West in 1869 on locomotive and railroad cars, and people loved to sing about railroads. In
Chapter II are "Echo Canyon," "The Utah Iron Horse," "The Railroad Cars They're Coming," and "The Iron Horse." In Chapter V
is "Zack, the Mormon Engineer." Other significant railroad songs
in my collection are "Casey Jones," "The Wreck of Number 9,"
"Wreck of the Old 97," "The Wabash Cannonball," and "Just Set
a Light."

Mormons sang many well-known outlaw songs: "Jesse James,"
"Sam Bass," "Dick Turpin," and "Brennan on the Moor." A ver-
sion called "Brandon on the Moor," collected from F. S. Harris of
American Fork, has the Irish outlaw captured in Castle Dale (a
Utah town) by the F.B.I. The folk have nearly always thought of
their outlaws as heroes, and these outlaw songs sung by the Mor-

mons tell the story of the outlaw sympathetically. Dick Turpin may outwit his companion, may be a desperado, yet the folk see his good side—not only his wit and courage, but also his acts of kindness. Don Wakefield gave me a version of "Bonny Black Bess," a song about Dick Turpin's horse, in which Turpin shows sentimental love for the beautiful animal. While singing the song for recording, Wakefield was so touched with sentiment that tears sprang into his eyes and his voice cracked.

Mormons usually have big families; therefore, children's songs are popular among them. In my collection are dozens of songs for children of all ages. There are lullabies such as "The Evening Train," contributed by L. M. Hilton:

> The first train leaves at six P.M.
> For the land where poppies grow.
> The mother dear is the engineer
> And each passenger laughs and crows.
> The palace car is the mother's arms,
> The whistle, the low, sweet strain,
> The passengers wink and nod and blink,
> And go to sleep on the train.

And there are songs with rollicking humor and nonsense refrains such as the following from a version of "Froggie Went a Courtin'," contributed by Bob Chistmas:

> Keemi Kimo, in the land of faro faro,
> Come a rat trap tenny-winkle,
> Tommy-doodle, rattle bugger,
> Rat trap tenny, won't you kime me oh.

There are talking birds and animals, carrion crows, Jolly Old Saint Nick, Molly O'Grady, Old Dan Tucker, Aunt Betsy, Daddy Grimes, and others.

A brief view of Mormon belief and custom regarding marriage, children, and family life shows what might be a theological basis for Mormon interest in children's songs. Theology of the Church of Jesus Christ of Latter-day Saints accepts as a part of the faith an existence of mankind before life on earth: at birth a spirit comes from the realm of the unborn and joins the body to become a living soul. Brigham Young, preaching in Salt Lake City, said:

There are multitudes of pure and holy spirits waiting to take taber-nacles; now what is our duty? To prepare tabernacles for them; to take a course that will not tend to drive those spirits into the families of the wicked, where they will be trained in wickedness, debauchery, and every species of crime. It is the duty of every righteous man and woman to prepare tabernacles for all the spirits they can. . . .

This is the reason why the doctrine of plurality of wives was revealed, that the noble spirits which are waiting for tabernacles might be brought forth.[20]

Supported by this theological concept, the Saints have always rejected birth control and emphasized family life. It is often said that children are Utah's best crop and so it is in marginal areas of southern Utah, where crops are sparse and families large.

The order of matrimony in the Church is marriage in the temple performed by the Priesthood "for time and all eternity." This ceremony is administered only to those who are judged to be worthy and eligible for admission to the "House of the Lord." Other members have a civil marriage for "time" only.

Hope for continuance of the marriage relationship after death and for the reuniting in eternity of family groups leads the Saints to give special attention to certain other practices regarding families. For example, babies and children are taken to church with the parents. Often Mormon church services seem noisy and irreverent, for babies cry and restlessly jostle with parents, and older children whisper. In the Sacrament Services, the most sacred meetings held on the Ward level, it is common to see father and mother sitting in a row with a whole family of children. Although something is lost in reverence through this practice, many Mormons "bear testimony" that religious faith and devotion are developed through families worshipping together.

In other practices regarding children Mormons are not unique. Like many other denominations, they emphasize religion in the home, family prayers, invocations for blessings and thanks at every meal, and home evenings with all the family together in worship and entertainment.

In the teachings of Joseph Smith and Brigham Young, however, patriarchal order was emphasized. For man to become like God, he must be father and patriarch of a family. Thus the doctrinal basis of the society imposes special attention to family life.

About one fifth of all the songs I have collected from Mormon folk are sentimental songs. Religious conviction and adoration for the Divine often come to those who are readily moved by emotion.

---

[20] John A. Widtsoe, ed., *Discourses of Brigham Young*, p. 305.

Even though its early leaders had great respect for learning and established schools for both children and adults, the Mormon Church is not highly intellectualized. The Church does not, however, engender or permit highly emotionalized revivals or conversions. Yet, as in most sects, appeals for attainment of faith through emotional conviction are uppermost. People are urged to meditate and pray for a "testimony of the truthfulness of the Gospel," and when they get it, to confess it before God. As a result of this and of the over-all pattern of worship, many followers acquire a dedication to religion that becomes an obsession. Monthly testimony meetings in every Ward bring many volunteers to their feet to declare with deep sincerity their faith and to give thanks to God for His kindness. The Church has no paid clergy on the Ward level; laity-operated without a trained ministry, the local church has few restraints on emotion. The Mormons can accept more tears of joy shed at testimony meetings; more idealistic parables, proverbs, and sayings; more personal advice and didactic discourses; more flattery of each other; more hyperbolic eulogies of the dead at funerals; and more sentiment in their lives than the tastes and digestion of many of their contemporaries can tolerate.

So, Mormons are sentimental people. In this antiromantic age when sentiment is subdued and sentimentality is abhorred, the Mormon society is out of step. This characteristic of the people accounts for their preserving hundreds of the melodramatic songs of the past days of sorrow and tears.

Among these songs are tearful songs of nostalgia. Thousands of Mormons have migrated to "Zion," and in doing so brought with them a communicable homesickness. It is not only fitting but inevitable that they should bring to their repertory songs of longing for Texas, Savannah, the sunny South, Dublin Bay, Erin on the Rhine, and for many other places where Mormons have lived.

My own mother and stepfather, Mormon folksingers themselves with an ebullience of sentiment, sang in our home, on evenings before World War I, parts or all of many sentimental songs. They had learned them in their youth from their associates and forebears and had never written them down or seen them in print. I remember my own reactions to the songs: how moods of pathos engulfed me as they sang of death in "Fair Charlotte," "Poor Little Joe," and "The Ship that Never Returned." I loved to hear them sing "Just Set a Light," "Charles A. Guiteau," "Take Me Home," "Row Your

Boat," and "Curtains of Night." These songs charged me with emotion, made me weep or nostalgically yearn for something unknown. Yet two of their songs, "The Blind Child's Prayer" and "The Drunkard's Dream," were too hyperbolic for me, even as a child.

Although serious minded, idealistic, and sentimental, pioneer Mormons had a sense of humor; they could laugh at themselves and at others so heartily that they were often called the merry Mormons. In Utah they sang of such things as a man being a railroad engineer, a polygamist, and a bishop, and having a wife in every town that his Denver and Rio Grande road passed through. They sang of the incongruity of a man asking a girl to be his sixteenth wife and to accept a sixteenth part of his love, and of the miracle of a man being able to survive with more than one wife.

A universal trait manifest in the behavior of these people is the joy they experience laughing at incongruous behavior. This appears in the Mormon adaptation of verses to the well-known song "Mountain Dew," not included in this book, in which "the Bishop came by [to get some moonshine liquor] with a good alibi/ Saying his wife had come down with the flu." This is doubly ironic since total abstinence from use of alcoholic beverages is expected of all Mormons.

Humorous songs not related to local events (and therefore not published herein) made up a large part of the repertory of Mormon singers. Many of the comic songs they sang were satiric, and the target for some of the satire was women. From the time of Petronius to the present, men have enjoyed shooting shafts of wit and satire at women, and women have not always been unwilling receivers.

Some songs I have collected which are aimed at women and the foibles against which they are directed are "At the Matinee" (shrewish flirtation), "I Had But Fifty Cents" (gluttony, gold digging), "I Can't Change It" (ugliness, deception), "Just Thirty-Five" (woman taking the man's role, man forced to take the woman's), "I Wish I Was Single" and "Bald Head End of the Broom" (marriage and the cantankerous wife), "Woman, Naughty Woman (troublemaking, extravagance, and selfishness).

Several of the best humorous songs deal with lack of elasticity, absentmindedness, or acting without thinking or in opposition to custom. In "The Mustard Plaster" the wife acts like an automaton. In "Corduroy" a boy's misfortune with his new pants is a result of absentmindedness or rigidity in failing to adjust quickly to a new emergency. In "Key Hole in the Door" the young Peeping Tom totally forgets himself and the superficiality of sophistication, thereby surrendering to emotion in single-minded absorption in what he sees. This song may be a descendant of the fragment, "The Whummil Bore" (Child 27), in which a man works for the king for seven years and sees the king's daughter but once and that through the whummil bore. Another likely descendant and a related one is that recorded by the hillbillies in the 1940's as "The Old Knot Hole."

I collected the song from F. S. Harris of American Fork, Utah, in August 1959.

Key Hole in the Door

O, when we left the parlor, I think 'twas scarcely nine,
And by some lucky fortune her room was next to mine;
Resolved like bold Columbus new regions to explore,
I took a snug position by the key hole in the door.

Chorus:
The key hole in the door, the key hole in the door,
I took a snug position by the key hole in the door.

Fair Jennie first proceeded, took off her pretty dress,
Likewise some underclothing, some fifty more or less.
To tell the truth sincerely, I think there was a score,
But I could not count correctly through the key hole
  in the door.

Chorus:
The key hole in the door, the key hole in the door,
I could not count correctly through the key hole in
  the door.

Then down upon the carpet she sat with graceful ease
And pulled some spotless linen above her snow-white knees;
A dainty sky-blue garter on either leg she wore,
It was a glowing picture through a key hole in the door.

Chorus:
The key hole in the door, the key hole in the door,
It was a glowing picture through the key hole in the
  door.

Then up before the fire her little feet to warm,
With nothing but a shimmy to hide her lovely form.
Said I, "Take off that shimmy, and I'll ask for nothing
  more."
And you bet I saw her do it through the key hole in
  the door.

Chorus:
The key hole in the door, the key hole in the door,
You bet I saw her do it through the key hole in the
    door.

Then up before the mirror this pretty damsel stood—
Viewing her rich beauty, fever in my blood.
My heart it beat with rapture as never known before;
In truth I felt like jumping through the key hole in
    the door.

Chorus:
The key hole in the door, the key hole in the door,
In truth I felt like jumping through the key hole in
    the door.

Then down upon the pillow she laid her dainty head.
The light was extinguished, and darkness hid the bed.
I thought the show was over, no use to admire more,
So my post I abandoned by the key hole in the door.

Chorus:
The key hole in the door, the key hole in the door.
So my post I abandoned by the key hole in the door.

Now all you men of science, don't strain your eager eyes
Viewing the planets that deck the distant skies,
For nature has more wonders than all you could explore;
A telescope is nothing to the key hole in the door.

Chorus:
The key hole in the door, the key hole in the door,
A telescope is nothing to the key hole in the door.

With this group appear many songs in which wit and surprise
are the basis of the humor. In "The Old Arm Chair" the useless
legacy of the chair becomes a valuable depository of unexpected
money—to the happiness of the storyteller and the chagrin of his
taunters. In "Give Him One More as He Goes" the good-night kiss
from the sweetheart becomes a good-night kick from the father and
a good-night bite from the dog. In "The Lawyer Outwitted" the legal
advice given by the lawyer becomes the lawyer's trap and the young
man's triumph in getting the daughter. The element of surprise is
the basic source of humor in the stories presented in "The Derby
Ram," "Whoa, Mule, Whoa," and "Finnegan's Wake."

All of these songs which Mormons have gathered from others
and used for their amusement were the typical subjects for laughter
of a few generations ago both in and out of Mormondom.

Many songs Mormons sing came from the British Isles along with

British Mormons. In my collection are twelve versions of Child ballads as well as other transplants showing English origin. They vary from the murder story of "Lady Isabel and the Elf Knight" to humorous derivatives of serious ballads. Such a ballad is "The Old Shoe." This song and its counterpart in Child, "The Marriage of Sir Gawain" (31), for example, have the same motif—a beautiful lady of high rank is thought by a lover to be most distasteful but is transformed while in bed to her true self. From the old to the new two changes are most noticeable: the sex story is softened in tone, and the supernatural element of a person being under the power of a stepmother witch is eliminated. The ballad is changed in character, setting, plot, and narrative to make a plausible story without supernatural elements and without violation of Victorian taboos in sex narrative.

Mrs. Eliza Jane Avery, of Burley, Idaho, sang this entire song to me about 1930. She was feeble and old then, but able to sing this and many other songs with dramatic energy:

The Old Shoe

'Tis of an old man in Plymouth did dwell
And he had a daughter, a beautiful girl;
A young man, he courted her to be his bride;
This plentiful fortune encumbered her pride,
    Encumbered her pride.

He courted her long and gained her love,
But still she intended this young man to prove;
One day he said to her, and thus she replied,
She told him right there she would ne'er be his bride,
    She would ne'er be his bride.

Then hearing those sad words from his dear;
'Twas with a sad oath, oh then, he did swear
That he'd have the first woman that e'er he did see,
If she was mean as a beggar could be,
    As a beggar could be.

She ordered her servants this young man to delay
While she her rich jewels had all put away;
Then she dressed herself up in the worst she could find;
She looked like old Cheepi, before and behind,
    Before and behind.

She rubbed her hands on the chimney jam,
She rubbed her face from corner to chin,
And down the road she ran like a witch

With her petticoat hoisted all on a half hitch,
    All on a half hitch.

Then as he came riding, and thus he did see her;
It was for his sad oath, oh then, he did fear,
With her old shoe heel jammed down to ascrew,
He soon overtook her and says, "Who are you?"
        And says, "Who are you?"
"I'm a woman."

This answer, it struck him as well as a dead man,
He stumbled, he staggered, he hardly could stand.
"Oh, how can I fear for to have you?" said he.
And then he soon asked her, saying: "Will you have me?"
        Saying: "Will you have me?"
"Yes, I will."

This answer, it suited as well as the rest,
But lay very heavy and sore on his breast,
'Twas for his oath's sake he must make her his bride,
And then he soon asked her behind him to ride,
        Behind him to ride.
"Your horse will throw me; I know it will."

"Oh, no! Oh, no! My horse, it will not."
She mustered around and behind him she got.
"My heart it doth fail me, I dare not go home,
My parents will say I'm forever undone,
        I'm forever undone."

He took her to neighbors, with whom he was great;
'Twas of his sad story he dare not relate.
"It's here with my neighbors a while you will tarry,
And in a short time I with you will marry,
        I with you will marry."
"You won't! I know you won't!"

He told her he would, and home he did go;
He told his father and mother also,
And of his sad case and how he had sworn.
"All's well," said his parents, and they did not mourn,
        And they did not mourn.

"Son, break not your vows, but bring home your girl,
And we'll fix her up so she'll do very well."
So published they were, and invited the guests,
And they intended the bride for to dress,
        The bride for to dress.
"I'll wear my old clothes as I used to."

Then he invited his old spark to come;
Her servants replied, "She is not at home."

He ordered his servants to wait on her there,
And then for the wedding they all did prepare,
  They all did prepare.

And when they were married and sat down to eat,
With her fingers she clawed out the cabbage and meat,
And in the hot pudding she burned them to fags;
She licked them and wiped them all on her old rags,
  All on her old rags.

Then faster endeavor, she at it again,
They all laughed in private 'til their sides ached
  with pain;
Then while they were stopped some called her his bride,
Saying, "Go, you love, do and sit down by his side,
  Sit down by his side."
"I'll sit in the corner as I used to."

Some, they were tickled and very much pleased,
While others were sorry and very much grieved;
They gave her a candle, what could she ask more?
And showed her the way to her chamber door,
  To her chamber door.
"Husband, when you hear my old shoe go, 'clung,' then,
you can come."

Upstairs she went and kept stepping about;
His Mother says, "Son, what think you the row?"
"Oh, Mother! Dear Mother, don't say one word,
For no more comfort may this world me afford,
  May this world me afford."

And by and by the old shoe it went, "clung";
They gave him a candle and bade him go along.
"I choose for to go in the dark," then he said,
"For I very well know the way to my bed,
  The way to my bed."

He jumped in his bed with his back to his bride,
She rolled, and she tumbled from pillow to side,
And as she turned over, the bed it did squeak.
"What the devil's the matter? Why don't you lay still?
  Why don't you lay still?"
"My shins are sore, I want a candle to dress them by."

He called for a candle to dress his wife's shins,
And found she was clothed in the finest of things;
And as she turned over, her face to behold,
He found she was fairer than pictures of gold,
  Than pictures of gold.

"Is it you? Is it you?" with his arms around her waist.
The answer was "Yes," and they all came in haste;

They looked like two pictures that pleased the eye,
And through many a fair glass we wish them much joy.
We wish them much joy.

As for artistry in words and music of songs Mormons have composed, some further observations may be made. Wording is in general commonplace, the words used by common men. The inclination toward hymns, ballads, and sentimental songs is characteristic of the people. There is little originality in musical aspects; the folk for the most part used familiar, borrowed tunes. The Church's traditional emphasis on music led to such singing without restraint that other folk dubbed the Mormons the "Singing Saints."

The problem of distinguishing between faith and folly, between truth in faith and falsehood in superstition, which is an eternal problem with the folklorist, is especially acute with students of Mormon folklore. It is hard to distinguish in various aspects the theology of the official hierarchy from that of the untutored flock. Their songs reflect the faith of the people and their folly.

Most native Mormon folksong, like much native American balladry, is based on historical fact.[21] Ballads are surprisingly accurate accounts of dramatic events. Songs are especially distinctive in accuracy in presenting Mormon history, customs, and thinking. An examination of the songs in this book and the accompanying accounts of history, customs, and doctrines will reveal this close relationship.

[21] See G. Malcolm Laws, Jr., *Native American Balladry from British Broadsides*, Chapter V.

Songs Dealing with Mormon History

The Church of Jesus Christ of Latter-day Saints, popularly called the Mormon Church, originated with Joseph Smith, Jr., who was born in Sharon, Vermont, in 1805, and killed by a mob on June 27, 1844, in Carthage, Illinois. Organized in 1830, the Church now has about two million members, most of whom live in the western part of the United States, and has its center of operations in Salt Lake City, Utah. It has Stakes and Missions in many other parts of the world.

Establishment of the Church was preceded by several important events in the life of its young founder, Joseph Smith. When he was ten years old, the family moved to western New York, and Joseph grew up on a farm between Palmyra and Manchester in the vicinity of Rochester.

The religious attitude of this portion of the country during Joseph's youth was violent and fanatical. Crossed and recrossed by revival preachers, it had become so wrought up emotionally that it was known as the "burnt over" district. Within it a multitude of conflicting sects competed for the attention and the loyalty of a roving and rootless population.[1]

Presbyterians, Methodists, and Baptists solicited for membership. New sects emerged: the Shakers, the Millerites, the Universal Friends, the Disciples of Christ. During a particular revival led by Reverend Mr. Stocton of the Presbyterian Church, Joseph's mother, his two brothers Hyrum and Samuel Harrison, and his sister Sophronia joined that church. His father remained unattached.

The fourteen-year-old Joseph was "much wrought up in spirit, and became 'somewhat partial' to the Methodist sect, and he 'felt a

---

[1] Ray B. West, *Kingdom of the Saints*, p. 14.

desire to be united with them.' "[2] He interpreted differences of revi-
valists as confusion and reasoned that God could not be author of
confusion. As the revival drew to a close, the Reverend Mr. Lane of
the Methodist Church gave a sermon on the subject, "Which
Church Shall I Join?" He quoted James 1:5: "If any of you lack
wisdom, let him ask of God that giveth to all men liberally and
upbraideth not, and it shall be given him." The passage deeply im-
pressed Joseph and, accordingly, he asked God for wisdom. The result of this prayer is recorded by the Church historian:

And now something strange happened. The youth had just begun
timidly to express the desire of his heart in words, when he was seized
upon by an invisible power that overcame him; his tongue was bound
so he could not speak. Darkness gathered around him, and it seemed for
a time that he was doomed to sudden destruction. He exerted all his
powers to call upon God for deliverance from this enemy—not from a
merely "imaginary ruin," as he assures us, "but from the power of
some actual being never before encountered." Despair seized him, and
he felt that he must abandon himself to destruction. At this moment of
dreadful alarm he saw a pillar of light exactly over his head which
shone out above the brightness of the sun, and began gradually descend-
ing toward him, until he was enveloped within it. As soon as the light
appeared, the youth found himself freed from the power of the enemy
that had held him bound. As the light rested upon him, he beheld within it two personages, exactly resembling each other in form and fea-
tures, standing above him in the air. One of these, calling Joseph by
name, and pointing to the other, said: "This is My Beloved Son, hear
Him. . . ."

It gives evidence of the intellectual tenacity of Joseph Smith that in
the midst of all these bewildering occurrences he held clearly in his
mind the purpose for which he had come to this secluded spot, the
object he had in view in seeking the Lord. As soon, therefore, as he
could get sufficient self presence he asked the Personages in whose re-
splendent presence he stood, which of the sects was right, and which
he should join. He was answered that he must join none of them; for
they were all wrong. [3]

He said he was told that he should prepare himself for an important work that he would be called to do, the nature of which would
be revealed to him in the future.

Three and a half years passed without further manifestations.
Joseph reported that he began to wonder when the Lord would carry
out His avowed purposes and establish the fulness of the Gospel on

[2] B. H. Roberts, *A Comprehensive History of the Church,* I, 52.
[3] *Ibid.,* I, 52–54.

earth. Then one night after the family had retired he again voiced a supplication and prayer:

While I was thus in the act of calling upon God, I discovered a light appearing in my room, which continued to increase until the room was lighter than at noonday, when immediately a personage appeared at my bedside, standing in the air, for his feet did not touch the floor. He had on a loose robe of most exquisite whiteness. . . .

When I first looked upon him I was afraid; but the fear soon left me. He called me by name and said unto me that he was a messenger sent from the presence of God to me and that his name was Moroni; that God had a work for me to do; and that my name should be had for good and evil among all nations, kindreds, and tongues, or that it should be both good and evil spoken of among all people. He said that there was a book deposited, written upon gold plates, giving an account of the former inhabitants of this continent, and the sources from which they sprang. He also said that the fulness of the everlasting Gospel was contained in it, as delivered by the Savior to the ancient inhabitants. [4]

Joseph's account goes on to tell in some detail subsequent events —where the plates were hidden, how they were to be translated by use of a *Urim and Thummin*, how the Gospel was re-established in its fulness through modern revelation, how Joseph was to get the gold plates and translate them, how the angel quoted biblical prophecy supporting modern revelation and restoration of the Gospel. He says that the angel returned twice more the same night and repeated the same message, that the angel appeared again the next day and told him to tell his father of the visions, that he went to the field where his father was working and told him, and that his father said it was of God. Then Joseph said that he left the field and went as the angel directed to the place where the plates were hidden; that on the hill called Cumorah he found the place of deposit, a stone box, and saw in it the plates and translating stones but was refused the right to take possession by the angel who stood by and told him that he should return to that spot in one year. He returned each year until he received the plates four years later, on September 22, 1827. His translation was published as the *Book of Mormon* on March 18, 1830. Less than a month later, on April 6, 1830, the Church was organized.

The appearance of the *Book of Mormon* alerted the religious world to the new religion—new, but founded, as its leaders avowed, on the

[4] Joseph Smith, Jr., *History of the Church of Jesus Christ of Latter-day Saints*, I, 12–15.

Bible, the *Book of Mormon,* and modern revelation. The *Book of Mormon,* according to Mormon faith, is both historical and doctrinal, giving an account of the rising and extermination of ancient American civilizations and presenting sermons and teachings of religious leaders of those civilizations. The new book gave prominence to several ideas—happiness is obtained through righteous living; wickedness, interpreted as turning away from God, brings misery, disaster, and destruction. It emphasized continued revelation:

And again I speak unto you, who deny the revelations of God and say that they are done away, that there are no revelations, nor prophecies, nor gifts, nor healing, nor speaking with tongues and the interpretation of tongues. Behold I say unto you, he that denieth these things knoweth not the Gospel of Christ. (Mormon 9:7–8)

The new Church grew rapidly; its converts were zealous, its leaders fearless. In face of ridicule and persecution it prospered, even though the group found it expedient, desirable, or necessary to establish homes in new areas from time to time. Church leaders turned toward the West, where a promise of isolation meant security to establish what they termed the Kingdom of God. Thus they moved first to Ohio, thence to Missouri, and then, forcefully expelled from Missouri, to Illinois—only to be driven out again; this time they were not to stop until they reached the intermountain West.[5]

ᖉᖆᑯ 1. *The Story of Mormonism* ᖉᖆᑯ

L. M. Hilton learned this song from his grandfather, Joseph W. McMurrin, who was ordained one of the Seven Presidents of Seventies[6] at the age of thirty-nine and served in that capacity for thirty-four years until his death in 1932. Mr. Hilton says that the music, published herewith, is that of an old song, "O'er the Lea." Although he claims that the song has been sung in various areas in the Church, I have not found it in any other collection. Mr. McMurrin also sings the song to the tune of "Marching Through Georgia" and adds the

---

[5] For a detailed account of this period of Mormon history, see Roberts, *A Comprehensive History of the Church,* Vols. I, II, III.

[6] A Priesthood office, one of twenty-six general authorities of the Church. A major duty of one holding this office is to supervise missionary work.

same chorus as that in Song No. 47. This type of amalgamation of two songs is not uncommon in folk practice.

Sung by L. M. Hilton, Ogden, Utah, July 18, 1959.

1. *The Story of Mormonism*

We've heard fantastic tales for years
About the Mormon nation
And Utah's wonderland of birth
And courage in creation.
There does not seem to be on earth
A subject more entrancing
Than Mormonism and the Saints
And how they are advancing,
And how they are advancing,
And how they are advancing,

Than Mormonism and the Saints
And how they are advancing.

We used to hear they all had horns,[7]
With barbs their tails were ended,
That each man had a score of wives
To keep his trousers mended.
These minor points I'll now pass by,
We'll take them up in order
And get the general run of facts
That now are in disorder.

The Mormon faith was founded by
A man whose early teaching
Along old Presbyterian lines
Was famous for such preaching.
Vermont produced a boy who gave
The world a new religion,
A boy who played like other boys
And owned a dog and pigeon.

This boy by name was Joseph Smith,
At first engaged in farming,
Whose Presbyterian father's faith
Had never been alarming.
With Joseph fourteen years of age
The family started moving
And settled first in New York State
Where times were fast improving.

About that time religion grew
To be a thing disputed;
Beliefs were challenged right and left,
Defended and refuted.
Young Joseph listened ill at ease,
His ideas quite divided
Until the Lord to him appeared
And left him more decided.

---

[7] Just how the lore of Mormons having horns arose is a matter of conjecture, but Professor Carl E. Young and others believe that it is derived from the ancient tradition that a cuckold grew horns. If a man had many wives, as some Mormon men did, then surely he would be made a cuckold and would grow horns.

The young man vowed the Lord of Hosts
A neutral ground demanded
Regarding all religious views
Until his mind expanded.
He told his friends the Lord had said
Their faiths were wrongly founded
And warned him to beware of all
Lest he should be confounded.

Through either envy or chagrin
His closest friends reviled him
And persecuting him for faith,
Vision-gazer they styled him.
In eighteen hundred twenty-three,
Age eighteen years or under,
Young Joseph had a second call
That filled his soul with wonder.

This time an angel did appear
In gleaming robes of glory,
Who told the young man standing there
A weird and wondrous story.
He told him where upon a hill
A box of stone was buried,
In which he'd find some golden plates
And other objects varied.

The angel then revealed himself
The messenger of standing,
Moroni, son of Mormon sent
The Saints to be commanding.
Then three times more the angel came
To Joseph in a vision
To tell him more about the plates
And learn of his decision.

The time arrived to view the plates,
And Joseph soon was kneeling
Beside the stone the angel said
The treasures were concealing.
Removing this, he found the plates
And then to his elation

The *Urim* and the *Thummin* found
To aid him in translation.

The angel then told Joseph Smith
That four more years were needed
Before he might remove the plates,
And this the boy conceded.
Four years then rolled slowly by,
And meanwhile Joseph married
But took good care that no one learned
The secret that he carried.

The angel then presented him
The plates, but stipulated
Their safe return as soon as he
Their message had translated.
A man named Cowdry then appeared
To aid him in transcribing
The story that the plates contained
And also the describing.

Together there the two men toiled
Upon their great translation.
The *Book of Mormon* was produced
And caused a great sensation.
It told a tale of scattered tribes
From Israel disbanded
Were gathered in America
As prophecies demanded.

The Nephites and the Lamanites
Their wars and homes defending
Upon the southern continent
And in the north there ending.
The tale of ancient wanderings
Philosophy and teachings
Soon thrilled the minds of young and old,
Its call was most beseeching.

The Church of Jesus Christ was formed
To purge the world of sinning.
The Saints of latter-day they called
Themselves since the beginning.

The new religion spread abroad
And met much approbation
But here at home its destiny
Was years of tribulation.

In fact the persecution forced
In time the Saints' removal
To what was then the frontier state
To still meet disapproval.
The anti-Mormon feeling rose
Against them in Missouri
To beckoning Illinois they went
To get beyond its fury.

'Twas here that Joseph met his fate,
A true religious martyr,
Determined that his soul at least
The cursers could not barter.
The murdered Prophet's death was mourned
By Saints throughout the nation,
Then Brigham Young was chosen chief
To lead their emigration.

The story of their western flight
Needs here no repetition.
They settled with their faith secure
From outside competition.
They colonized in Utah's vales
And built a wondrous city
That's grown into a commonwealth
As healthy as it's pretty.

2. Tittery-Irie-Aye

Since this song was collected by the Fifes in 1946, its popularity seems to have increased. The jogging rhythm of the lyrics fittingly emphasizes the words, especially in the line, "And they'll soon be a-packing up and jogging on their way." Joseph H. Watkins, an eighty-five year old singer from Brigham City, Utah, who sang it for the Fifes, gives special emphasis to the rhythm—a fact known by the many folklorists who have heard this song on the Library of Congress record "Songs of the Mormons" (AAFL LC 30).

Text and music from Austin and Alta Fife, Saints of Sage and Saddle, *pp. 318–319.*

Other sources: 67 Emrich; 68 Fife MCI, 592 (1946); 69 Columbia Records; 71 Sorrels and Fife.

2. *Tittery-Irie-Aye*

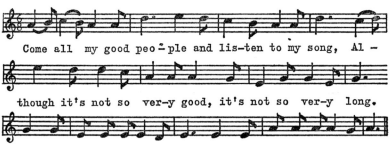

Come all my good peo-ple and lis-ten to my song, Although it's not so ver-y good, it's not so ver-y long.
And sing tit-te-ry-i-rie-aye, and sing tit-te-ry-i-rie-o.

Come all my good people and listen to my song,
Although it's not so very good, it's not so very long.

Chorus:
And sing tittery-irie-aye, and sing tittery-irie-o

Now concerning this strange people I'm now a-going
to sing,
For the way they have been treated I think it is a sin.

They've been driven from their homes and away from
Nauvoo
For to seek another home in the wilderness anew.

Oh, they stopped among the Indians but there don't
mean to stay,
And they'll soon be a-packing up and jogging on their
way.

They made a halt at Council Bluffs but there don't
mean to stay,
Some feed their cattle rushes and some prairie hay.

Oh, of logs we've built our houses, of dirt we have
    our floors,
Of sods we've built our chimneys and shakes we have
    for doors.

There is another item, to mention it I must
Concerning spiritual women that make a hell of a fuss.

Some men have got a dozen wives and others have a score,
And the man that's got but one wife is a-looking out
    for more.

Now young men, don't get discouraged, get married
    if you can,
But take care don't get a woman that belongs to
    another man.

Now concerning this strange people I have nothing
    more to say
Until we all get settled in some future day.

3. Campaign for General Smith

In the Mormon society obedience to authority became a most important mark of religious fervor. Inordinate group loyalty developed into a solidarity and exclusiveness which tended to arouse hatred and envy among nonmembers. Economically, socially, and politically the Mormons acted as a unit. The special privileges granted by the Nauvoo Charter did not please the outsiders when Nauvoo in 1844 became the largest city in Illinois. Since politically Mormons voted as a bloc, they could swing an election and thus were a strategic part of state politics.

Early in 1844, an election year, Joseph Smith wrote to the leading aspirants to the United States Presidency, Henry Clay and John C. Calhoun, asking them what pledges of protection they would offer the Mormons if they were elected. Both wrote evasive answers. Joseph, in a gesture of disgust, announced that he would himself be a candidate for President. He promptly asked for volunteer missionaries to travel throughout the states organizing his campaign, and 344 men offered their services. There is little reason to believe he had hope for success, but he wanted to test the power of the Church in political strength and to spread about his political philosophy.

The plan was interrupted and concluded by the death of the candidate. In the eyes of his followers the murder of Joseph Smith at the hands of a mob made him a martyr to the cause of Christian faith. Reasons for the mob action are numerous. Old enemies from Missouri, harboring a grudge, still pursued the Mormon leader. Mormon solidarity worried politicians. Mormon proselyting irritated ministers of other denominations. But the element of society which initiated the murder came from within the Church. William Law, Wilson Law, Robert D. Foster, Charles A. Foster, and others of influence in Nauvoo charged Joseph Smith with fraudulent speculation in real estate, with instituting licentious living in the Church through polygamous marriages, and with unfair and autocratic leadership. Joseph Smith called a council meeting and excommunicated the leaders of this faction without a hearing. They retaliated on June 7, 1844, by printing and circulating a paper, *The Nauvoo Expositor*, which exposed Joseph as a fallen prophet. Promptly Joseph called a council meeting and the council commissioned the Nauvoo Legion to burn the undistributed papers and destroy the press. When the order was executed, the fiery indignation of the enemies of the Prophet arose and they cried for revenge. Time-honored freedom of the press had been violated. In Warsaw and other neighboring towns mobs formed which threatened to sack Nauvoo. To protect his people General Joseph Smith (his title in the Nauvoo Legion) called the Legion and declared martial law in the city. This resulted in the arrest of Joseph Smith for treason and in his incarceration in the jail of the neighboring city of Carthage. Mob spirit running high, Joseph and his brethren asked for protection and Governor Ford stationed fifty men of the Carthage Grays to guard the jail. Because these men were avowed enemies of the Prophet, his friends became alarmed and petitioned the Governor to make a change, which he refused to do.

Later about seventy-five men from neighboring towns attacked the jail. The Carthage Grays offered no resistance. Action was quick. Hyrum Smith, brother of Joseph, fell with the first volley of shots fired and Joseph was shot as he attempted to jump from the window; John Taylor was seriously injured and the fourth member of the imprisoned group, Willard Richards, remained unhurt.

Thus the short-lived campaign of Joseph Smith for President of the United States was concluded. One hundred and thirty-five men had gone out as missionary campaigners to put the Prophet's political views before the people. My own grandfather, Shepherd Pierce Hutchings, was one of these. He had arrived in Ohio and had begun his campaign when the shattering news reached him and terminated his efforts. These short fragments of folksong treat this part of Mormon history.

Text from Levette J. Davidson, "Mormon Songs," Journal of American Folklore, *LVIII (October–December, 1945), 277.*

A

Kinderhoos, Kass, Kalhoun, or Klay
Kan never surely win the day.
But if you want to know who kan,
You'll find in General Smith, the man.

B

Come, then, O Americans rally to the standard of Liberty,
And in your generous indignation, trample down
The tyrant's rod and the oppressor's crown
That yon proud eagle to its height may soar
And peace, triumphant, reign forever more.[8]

⚮ *4. Mormon Battalion Song* ⚮

This song and the five songs which follow treat an important episode of Mormon history, the experiences of the Mormon Battalion. In 1846, two years after the martyrdom of Joseph Smith, the Mormons found it necessary because of persecution to leave Nauvoo, Illinois. Accordingly they crossed the Mississippi River and started toward the Rocky Mountains.

This same year establishment of a border line between the United States and Mexico brought the two countries into war. National leaders and President Polk, knowing that the Mormons were on the

---

[8] Davidson says: "The first is a stanza from a campaign song printed in *The Nauvoo Neighbor* and the second is from Parley Pratt's 'Smith for President.' Quoted by Harry M. Beardsley, *Joseph Smith and His Mormon Empire,* 320 and 337."

way to California or Oregon (names by which the western part of the United States was known), decided to make use of them to win the country. Five hundred men were called from the Mormon camps at Mount Pisgah and Council Bluffs. The Mormons responded, though to some people it appeared ironical that people who had been victims of persecutions from which the government had failed to protect them should respond to a government call.

The march of the Mormon Battalion from Iowa to the Mexican border and thence to the sea was said to have been unparralleled in recent history in the misery it produced,[9] though, considering the hardships of the handcart pioneers, this estimation must be taken as an exaggeration. No written account presents a better history of the hardships of these men than the songs composed and sung by them.

Levi Hancock, a folk artist who accompanied the troops on their long march, was one who composed many songs. He was forty-three years old at the time, had been a member of the Church since 1830, and was one of the First Council of Seventies. He was called by Brigham Young to be the spiritual advisor or chaplain to the group, though his official position was flutist in Company E. His songs were chiefly story songs of Battalion experiences.

Of the hardships and miseries the Battalion experienced, Evans says:

At last the weary and half-clad battalion reached the coast. They were congratulated by their leader, who declared that, though he had seen some dark days in his time, he had never even heard of anything like this journey. "History," he said, "may be searched in vain for an equal march of infantry." Half of it had been through a wilderness where nothing but savages and wild beasts are found, or deserts, where, for want of water, there is no living creature. . . . Without a guide who had traveled them, we have ventured into table lands where water was not found for several marches. . . . And General Kearny, when he heard the details of the march, said with great earnestness, "Bonapart crossed the Alps, but these men have crossed a continent."[10]

The Mormon Battalion never had to fight a battle. Their most serious encounter was with wild bulls, Texas longhorn cattle gone

[9] From a letter written to the Battalion on January 30, 1847, signed "By order Lieutenant Colonel P. St. George Cooke, P. C. Merrill, Adjutant" (Roberts, *A Comprehensive History of the Church*, I, 120).

[10] John Henry Evans, *One Hundred Years of Mormonism*, pp. 436–537.

wild. Indians had killed all young animals and cows for meat and had left the bulls.[11] Of the encounter with the bulls, Guy Keysor, private in Company B, wrote in his journal:

Two bulls came jumping into our marching column. One of them knocked down and ran over Sargeant Albert Smith bruising him severely. . . . Another couple of bulls raging with madness charged upon us. One of them tossed Amos Cox into the air and knocked down a pair of mules, goring one till his entrals hung out, which soon died. Cox wound was four inches long and three deep. . . . After advancing about half a mile another bull came rushing out of a muskeet [mesquite] thicket and charged upon the hind end of a wagon . . . but his career was short, for the command now had their muskets loaded.[12]

The contributor of this song says that it was composed by Eliza R. Snow after the Battalion boys returned home. She was one of Brigham Young's wives and a sister to Lorenzo Snow, who later became third president of the Church. A homespun poet, she composed songs and poems for many special occasions.

Daniel Tyler published (1881) a poem under the title "The Mormon Battalion, and First Wagon Road Over the Great American Desert." He assigns authorship to Eliza R. Snow. The version given here, arranged for singing, has five stanzas of ten lines each, but the poem has eighty-nine lines in eight stanzas, ranging in length from four lines to twenty-eight lines. Some striking lines omitted in the song are the following:

> Ere the Battalion started out
> Upon that most important route,
> 'Twas thus predicted by the tongue
> Of Apostle Brigham Young,
> "If to your God and country true,
> You'll have no fighting there to do."
> Was General Kearney satisfied?
> Yes, more—for he with martial pride
> Said, "O'er the Alps Napoleon went,
> But these men crossed a continent."[13]

---

[11] G. Malcolm Laws, Jr. lists this song as "The Buffalo Bull Fight" (*Native American Balladry*, p. 261). These were not buffalo but cattle gone wild. For verification, see the following: Roberts, *A Comprehensive History of the Church*, I, 114; Daniel Tyler, *A Concise History of the Mormon Battalion in the Mexican War*, p. 218; and Grant A. Golder, *March of the Mormon Battalion*, pp. 191 ff.

[12] Quoted by Golder, *March of the Mormon Battalion*, p. 193.

[13] Tyler, *A Concise History of the Mormon Battalion*, pp. 107–109.

Sung by L. M. Hilton, Ogden, Utah, July 18, 1959.

4. Mormon Battalion Song

When Mormon trains were journeying through
To Winter Quarters from Nauvoo,
Five hundred men were called to go
To settle claims with Mexico,
To fight for that same government
From which as fugitives we went.
What were our families to do,
Our children, wives, and mothers too?
When fathers, husbands, sons were gone
The dames drove teams and camp moved on.

And on the brave battalion went
With Colonel Allen who was sent,
And well old Colonel Allen knew
His Mormon boys were brave and true,
And he was proud of his command
As he led forth his Mormon band.
He sick and died and we were left,
Of a valiant leader soon bereaved,
And his successors proved to be
The embodiment of cruelty.

Lieutenant Smith, the tyrant, led
The battalion on in Allen's stead
To Santa Fe where Colonel Cook
The charge of our battalion took.
'Twas well the vision of the way
Was closed to us at Santa Fe
Because no infantry till then
Had ever suffered like us men.
Our rations gone long weeks before
We neared the great Pacific Shore.

Our teams fell dead upon the road;
Our soldiers had to pull the load.
We found road-making worse by far
Than all the horrors of the war.
The enemy was panic struck,
Dare not compete with Mormon pluck
And off in all directions fled;
No charge was fired, no blood was shed,
And Colonel Cook himself well knew
We Mormon men were brave and true.

Our God who rules in worlds by light
Controls by wisdom and by might.
The wise can see and understand
While fools ignore his guiding hand.
'Twas thus predicted by the tongue
Of our great leader, Brigham Young:
"If to your God and country true
You'll have no fighting there to do."

And thus with God Almighty's aid
The conquest and the roads were made.

☙ 5. *All Hail the Brave Battalion* ☙

Thomas Morris, private in Company E of the Battalion, is the composer of this song.

Sung by L. M. Hilton, Ogden, Utah, July 18, 1959.
Early copy: 23 Tyler 365 (1881).
Tune: "How Firm a Foundation," a Mormon hymn.

All hail the brave battalion, this noble valiant band,
We go to serve our country with willing heart and hand.
Although we're called disloyal by many a tongue and pen,
Our nation boasts no soldier, our nation boasts no soldier,
Our nation boasts no soldier, so true as Mormon men.

O'er many a barren desert our weary feet have trod
To find where unmolested the Saints may worship God.
We've built up many cities; we've built up Temples too
Which proves to all beholders, which proves to all beholders,
Which proves to all beholders, what Mormon hands can do.

We'll settle in the mountains upon a sterile soil
And by our faith and patience and hard unflinching toil
And through the daily blessing our Father, God, bestows
We'll make the barren desert, we'll make the barren desert,
We'll make the barren desert to blossom as the rose.

What though the wicked hate us and against our rights contend
And though their vile aggressions our brotherhood would rend,
The keys of truth and knowledge and power to us belong,
And we'll extend our borders, and we'll extend our borders,
And we'll extend our borders, and make our bulwark strong.

Our sons are growing mighty, indeed are spreading forth
To multiply our numbers and beautify the earth.
All hail the brave battalion, this noble valiant band,
We go to serve our country, we go to serve our country,
We go to serve our country, with willing heart and hand.

⚬⚬ 6. *The Desert Route* ⚬⚬

This song, like several others of this group, was written by Levi
Hancock of Company E of the Battalion.

*Contributed by Jenny Hancock, Provo, Utah, wife of a descend-
ant of Levi Hancock, November, 1959.*
Other source: 23 Tyler 182–183 (1881).

> While here beneath the sultry sky
> Our famished mules and cattle die,
> Scarce aught but skin and bones remain
> To feed poor soldiers on the plain.
>
> *Chorus:*
> How hard to starve and wear us out
> Upon this sandy desert route.
>
> Now half-starved oxen, over-drilled
> Too weak to draw, for beef are killed
> And gnawing hunger prompted men
> To eat small entrails and the skin.
>
> We sometimes now for lack of bread
> Are less than quarter rations fed,
> Then soon expect for want of meat
> Not less than broke-down mules to eat.
>
> Sometimes we quarter for the day
> While men are sent ten miles away
> On our back track to place in store
> An ox give out the day before.
>
> And when an ox is like to die
> The whole camp halts and we lay by;
> The greedy wolves and buzzards stay
> Expecting rations for the day.
>
> Our hardships reach their rough extremes
> When valiant men are roped with teams,
> Hour after hour and day by day,
> To wear our strength and lives away.
>
> The teams can hardly drag their loads
> Along the hills and sandy roads,

While traveling near the Rio Grande,
O'er hills and dales of heated sand.

We see some twenty men or more
With empty stomachs, and foot sore,
Bound to one wagon, plodding on
Through sand beneath the burning sun.

A doctor, which the government
Has furnished, proves a punishment;
At his rude call of "Jim along Joe,"
The sick and halt to him must go.

Both night and morn this call is heard;
Our indignation then is stirred.
And we sincerely wish in hell
His arsenic and his calomel.

To take it if we are not inclined,
We're threatened, "You'll be left behind."
When bored with threats profanely rough
We swallow down the poison stuff.

Some stand the journey well,
And some are by hardships overcome.
And thus the Mormons are worn out
Along this long and weary route.

7. The Bullfight on the San Pedro[14]

The composer of this as well as the preceding song was Levi Hancock of the Mormon Battalion's Company E. The story given here of a unique experience of the Mormon Battalion is accepted as an accurate account by historians. The strikingly good musical rhythm and the exciting and well-told narrative appeal to singers. It is among the most widely circulated Mormon songs. Rosalie Sorrels sang it for Dr. Fife on her record "Songs of the Mormon Pioneers." L. M. Hilton and Elayne Clark have sung it frequently in Mormon country. Few changes or corruptions appear in any versions I have examined.

[14] See footnote 11, p. 37.

Text and music from Jenny Hancock, Provo, Utah, November, 1959.

Other sources: 23 Tyler 221–223; 39 Durham 142–143; 42 Fife 319; 43 Hubbard 447; 51 Laws 344; 67 Emrich; 68 Fife MC I, 742 (William T. Morris, St. George, Utah, 1947); 69 Columbia Records; 71 Sorrels and Fife.

7. The Bullfight on the San Pedro

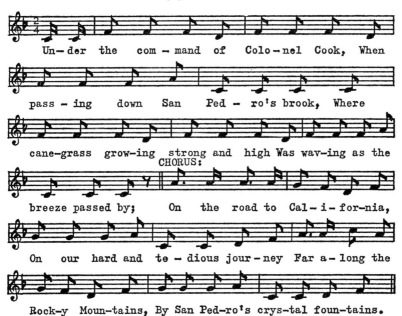

Under the command of Colonel Cook,
When passing down San Pedro's brook,
Where cane-grass growing strong and high
Was waving as the breeze passed by;
There as we gained ascending ground,
Out from the grass with fearful bound,
A wild ferocious bull appeared,
And challenged fight with horns upreared.

Chorus:
On the road to California,
On our hard and tedious journey

Far along the Rocky Mountains,
By San Pedro's crystal fountains.

"Stop, stop," said one, "Just see that brute."
"Hold," was responded, "Let me shoot."
He flashed but failed to fire the gun;
Both stood their ground and would not run.
The man explained, "I want some meat,"
And saying thus again he shot,
And felled the creature on the spot.

It soon arose to run away,
And then the guns began to play;
All hands at work amid the roar,
The bull was dropped to rise no more.
But lo, it did not end the fight—
A furious herd rushed into sight,
And then the bulls and men around
Seemed all resolved to stand their ground.

In nature's pasture, all unfenced,
A dreadful battle was commenced,
We knew ourselves we must defend,
And must to others aid extend.
The bulls with maddened fury raged,
The men with skillful warfare waged,
Though some from danger had to flee,
And hide or clamber up a tree.

A bull at one man made a pass,
Who hid himself amid the grass,
And breathless lay until the brute
Passed him and took another shoot.
The bulls rushed on like unicorns,
And gored the mules with piercing horns,
As if the battle ground to gain
When men and mules should all be slain.

With brutal strength and iron will,
Poised on his horns with master's skill,
A bull, one mule o'er mule did throw
Then made the latter's entrails flow.
One bull was shot and when he fell,

A butcher ran his blood to spill,
The bull threw up his horns and caught
The butcher's cap, upon the spot.

"Give up my cap," exclaimed the man,
And chased the bull as on he ran;
The butcher beat, and with his knife,
Cut the bull's throat and closed his life.
O, Cox from one bull's horn was thrown,
Ten feet in air; when he came down,
A gaping flesh wound met his eyes
The vicious bull had gored his thigh.

The colonel and his staff were there,
Mounted and witnessing the war;
A bull one hundred yards away
Eyed Colonel Cook as easy prey.
But Corp'al Frost stood bravely by,
And watched the bull with steady eye;
The brute approached near, and more near,
But Frost betrayed no sign of fear.

The Colonel ordered him to run,
Unmoved he stood with loaded gun;
The bull came up with daring tread,
When near his feet, Frost shot him dead.
Whatever cause, we do not know,
But something prompted them to do;
When all at once in frantic fright
The bulls ran bellowing out of sight.

And when the fearful fight was o'er,
And sound of muscats heard no more,
At least a score of bulls were found
And two mules dead upon the ground.
On the road to California
On our hard and tedious journey,
Far along the Rocky Mountains
By San Pedro's crystal fountains.

8. *The Lonesome Roving Wolves*

The composer of this ballad, Levi Hancock, creates an encompassing, lonely mood as he tells of the death of a teamster, his last moans accompanied by the roar of high winds in the mountains and the howls of ravenous wolves.

Contributed by Jenny Hancock, Provo, Utah, November, 1959.
Other sources: 23 Tyler 216–217 (1881); 68 Fife MC I, 601, 739
(Noah Stone, Fillmore, 1945 and 1946); 71 Sorrels and Fife.

The battalion encamped, by the side of the grove,
Where the pure waters flowed from the mountains above,
Our brave hunters came in from the chase of wild bulls,
All around rose the din of the howling wolves.

When the guards were all placed on the out-posts around,
The low hills and broad waters were alive with the sound,
Though the cold wind blew down the huge mountain shelves,
All was rife with a cry of the ravenous wolves.

Thus we watched the last breath of the teamster who lay,
In the cold grasp of death as his life wore away,
In deep anguish he moaned as if mocking his pain;
When the dying man groaned, the wolves howled a refrain.

For it seemed the wolves knew there was death in the camp
As the tones louder grew, the more hurried their tramp,
While the dead lay within with our grief to the full,
O how horrid a din, was the howl of the wolves.

Then we dug a deep grave, and we buried him there
All alone by the road not a stone to tell where,
But we piled brush and wood and burned over his grave
As a cheat to delude both the savage and wolf.

'Twas a sad, doleful night; we by sunrise next day
When the fifes and the drums had performed reveille,
When the teams were brought nigh, our baggage to pull,
One and all bade goodbye to the grave and the wolves.

᏶ 9. *The Mormon Battalion Song* ᏶

Songs by men who served in the Battalion catch the folk spirit more accurately than does Eliza R. Snow, composer of Song No. 4. A Battalion private, Azariah Smith, composed this while quartered in San Diego.

Text from Daniel Tyler, A Concise History of the Mormon Battalion in the Mexican War *(1881) pp. 287–289.*

In forty-six we bade adieu
To loving friends and kindred too;
For one year's service, one and all
Enlisted at our country's call,
    In these hard times.

We onward marched until we gained
Fort Leavenworth, where we obtained
Our outfit—each a musket drew—
Canteen, knapsack, and money, too,
    In these hard times.

Our Colonel died—Smith took his place,
And marched us on at rapid pace;
O'er hills and plains, we had to go,
Through herds of deer and buffalo,
    In these hard times.

At length we came to Santa Fe,
As much fatigued as men could be;
With only ten days there to stay,
When orders came to march away,
    In these hard times.

Three days and twenty we march'd down
Rio Del Norte, past many a town;
Then changed our course—resolved to go
Across the mountains, high or low,
    In these hard times.

We found the mountains very high,
Our patience and our strength to try;
For, on half rations, day by day,

O'er mountain heights we made our way,
   In these hard times.

Some pushed the wagons up the hill,
Some drove the teams, some pack'd the mules,
Some stood on guard by night and day,
Lest haplessly our teams should stray,
   In these hard times.

We traveled twenty days or more,
Adown the Gila River's shore—
Crossed o'er the Colorado then,
And marched upon a sandy plain,
   In these hard times.

We thirsted much from day to day,
And mules were dying by the way,
When Lo! to view, a glad scene burst,
Where all could quench our burning thirst,
   In these hard times.

We traveled on without delay,
And quartered at San Luis Rey;
We halted there some thirty days,
And now are quartered in this place,
   In these hard times.

A "Mormon" soldier band we are:
May our great Father's watchful care
In safety kindly guide our feet,
Till we, again, our friends shall meet,
   And have good times.

O yes, we trust to meet our friends
Where truth its light to all extends—
Where love prevails in every breast,
Throughout the province of the blest,
   And have good times.

10. *The Camp of Israel*

The folk pattern of the Mormon social milieu is reflected in this song with its use of the terms Israel (for Mormons) and Gentiles (for non-Mormons) and in the obvious comparison of the exodus of the Mormons from Nauvoo to the exodus of ancient Israel from Egypt. The Lord of Hosts is guarding the front and rear as the Camp of Israel moves on.

Eliza R. Snow, always ready with her pen to write a song for a special occasion, often caught the spirit of folk thought as she does here.

Text from the Millennial Star, *May 15, 1848, p. 160.*

> Altho' in woods and tents we dwell,
> Shout, shout O Camp of Israel!
> No Gentile mobs on earth can bind
> Our thoughts, or steal our peace of mind.
>
> *Chorus:*
> Tho' oppression's waves roll o'er us,
>   We will praise our God and King;
> We've a better day before us—
>   Of that day we proudly sing.
>
> We'd better live in tents and smoke
> Than wear the cursed Gentile yoke;
> We'd better from our country fly
> Than by religious mobs to die.
>
> We've left the city of Nauvoo
> And our beloved Temple too;
> And to the wilderness we go
> Amid the winter frosts and snow.
>
> Our homes were dear, we lov'd them well;
> Beneath our roof 'twas sweet to dwell,
> And honour the great God's commands,
> By mutual rights of Christian lands.
>
> Our persecutors will not cease
> Their murderous spoiling of our peace;
> And for their hatred we must go
> To the wilds where reeds and rushes grow.

The Camp—the camp—it's numbers swell!
Shout, shout O Camp of Israel!
The King, the Lord of Hosts is near;
His armies guard our front and rear.

⤖ 11. *Whoa, Haw, Buck and Jerry Boy* ⤖

Evan Stephens, a former Tabernacle Choir leader of many years'
service, preserved this song. It was sung when he crossed the plains,
in the late 1850's, often providing music for dances. Although the
melody has little variety, Mr. Hilton, who learned it in his youth,
sings it with a vigor that has made it popular with his audiences.

Sung by L. M. Hilton, Ogden, Utah, July 18, 1959.
*Other sources: 69 Columbia Records 1965; 70 Hilton; 71 Sorrels
and Fife.*

11. *Whoa, Haw, Buck and Jerry Boy*

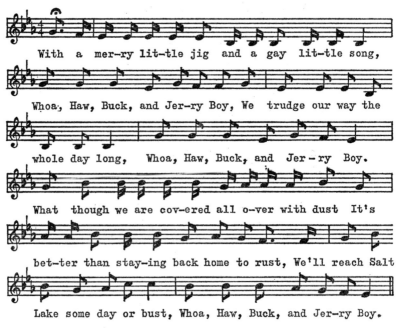

With a mer-ry lit-tle jig and a gay lit-tle song,
Whoa, Haw, Buck, and Jer-ry Boy, We trudge our way the
whole day long, Whoa, Haw, Buck, and Jer-ry Boy.
What though we are cov-ered all o-ver with dust It's
bet-ter than stay-ing back home to rust, We'll reach Salt
Lake some day or bust, Whoa, Haw, Buck, and Jer-ry Boy.

With a merry little jig and a gay little song,
Whoa, Haw, Buck, and Jerry Boy,
We trudge our way the whole day long,
Whoa, Haw, Buck, and Jerry Boy.
What though we are covered all over with dust
It's better than staying back home to rust,
We'll reach Salt Lake some day or bust,
Whoa, Haw, Buck, and Jerry Boy.

There's a pretty little girl in the outfit ahead,
Whoa, Haw, Buck, and Jerry Boy.
I wish she was by my side instead,
Whoa, Haw, Buck, and Jerry Boy.
Look at her now with a pout on her lips
As daintily with her finger tips
She picks for the fire some buffalo chips,
Whoa, Haw, Buck, and Jerry Boy.

Oh, tonight we'll dance by the light of the moon,
Whoa, Haw, Buck, and Jerry Boy.
To the fiddler's best and only tune,
Whoa, Haw, Buck, and Jerry Boy.
Holding her hand and stealing a kiss
But never a step of the dance we miss,
Never did know a love like this,
Whoa, Haw, Buck, and Jerry Boy.

☙ 12. *The Ox Team Trail* ❧

The words of this number provide significant local color, but the slow pace of the music to which the words are adapted is scarcely fitting to the movement suggested. Yet, Columbia Records used it nicely in their Legacy Record of the Mormons.

Sung by L. M. Hilton, Ogden, Utah, October, 1959.
Other source: 69 Columbia Records 1965.

12. *The Ox Team Trail*

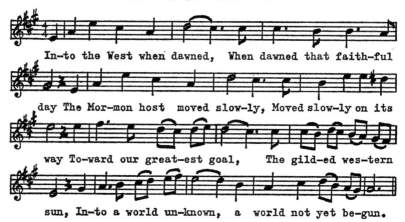

In-to the West when dawned, When dawned that faith-ful
day The Mor-mon host moved slow-ly, Moved slow-ly on its
way To-ward our great-est goal, The gild-ed wes-tern
sun, In-to a world un-known, a world not yet be-gun.

Into the West when dawned,
When dawned that faithful day
The Mormon host moved slowly,
Moved slowly on its way
Toward our greatest goal,
The gilded western sun,
Into a world unknown,
A world not yet begun.

Where barren sagebrush prairies
And hostile Indian hordes
Comprised the West's own welcome,
All it could then afford.
Our pioneers pressed forward,
Bound for a realm of peace
Where strife among the world,
The world and them might cease.

The rumble of the axles,
Stout axles built of oak,
The pant of beasts revealing
Their straining at the yoke,
The screams of brakes and children,
Of wagon beds and gear
Were mingled sounds with laughter
That listening ears might hear.

When twilight shades had cooled,
Had cooled the desert's breath,
Then camped these hosts of Israel
Upon that plain of death.
Their prayers arose from circles
Of faithful Saints drawn round
The campfires of these pilgrims,
These pilgrims western bound.

Then followed close each other
Along the winding trail
While summer's sweltering heat and
Mirages did prevail.
And hurricanes of dust
And awful frightening drought
Came rushing down upon them
From out the torrid South.

At each day's camp skull milestones
For those to come they'd leave,
Encouraging directions
That others might perceive.
Thus on and on they traveled
O'er rivers choked with ice
Where bloodstains marked the passage
To show they'd paid a price.

Now ox teams swimming rivers
To cross from shore to shore,
And people on large rafts
Just guided by an oar,
And bands of redskin beggars
Molesting through the day
Would steal at night and kill
When they were brought to bay.

Ere ending this journey
Through hunger, want, and pain,
The aged ones were dying
Along the wagon train.
New babies born of mothers,
To mothers gone tan pale,

Who prayerfully kept plodding
Along the Mormon Trail.

What grateful prayers are offered
At last as they descend
Into the mountain valleys
Which marked the journey's end,
Where few white men's feet
As yet had ever trod,
But where these pioneer pilgrims
Could live and worship God.

13. *The Way We Crossed the Plains*

The Captain Murdock referred to in this song is a man who was
commissioned to direct a wagon train from Salt Lake Valley east
to Council Bluffs, Iowa, to bring back a party of immigrants from
Europe. It appears that the song was composed by his party. Various
immigrant groups sang the song en route west. Now it is often
heard in pioneer celebrations.

Sung by M. E. Wakefield, Ogden, Utah, 1959.
Other source: 39 Durham 299.

In a shaky wagon we ride,
For to cross the prairie wide.
As slowly the oxen moved along,
We walloped them well with a good leather thong.

Chorus:
And that's the way,
The way we crossed the plains,
And the way we crossed the plains.

A noise is heard as if for battle,
When Captain Murdock says drive in the cattle.
They picked up their whips as if to excel,
As if they were driving them into corral.

We needed fire to fry the meat
To make it good for us to eat

When for fire we couldn't find any sticks
We had to build it with buffalo chips.

13. *The Way We Crossed the Plains*

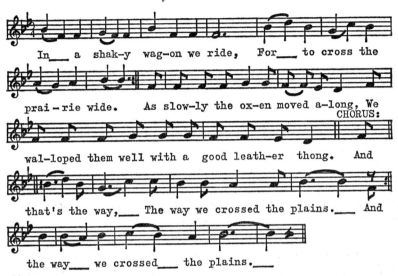

In___ a shak-y wag-on we ride, For___ to cross the

prai-rie wide. As slow-ly the ox-en moved a-long, We

CHORUS:

wal-loped them well with a good leath-er thong. And

that's the way,___ The way we crossed the plains.___ And

the way___ we crossed___ the plains.___

14. *Ye Elders of Israel*

This song catches especially well the attitude of the distinctive Mormon culture in 1857. It reflects the indoctrination of the new converts toward security in their new-found faith. Their joy in turning their backs on the world and "going to Zion" (being established in the Rocky Mountains) is also evident in the following quotation from the *Millennial Star* of April 11, 1857:

The splendid ship *George Washington,* bound for Boston, cleared off the 27th of March, having on board 817 souls of the Saints. . . . About 3 o'clock, p.m., the Saints were called together on the upper deck. . . . During the meeting several hymns suitable to the occasion were sung by the Brethren and Sisters in a spirited manner, one of which was—

"Ye elders of Israel, come join now with me," etc.,

with the chorus

"O Babylon, O Babylon, we bid thee farewell,
We're going to the Mountains of Ephraim to dwell."

All hearts seemed to be filled with joy, peace, and praise to their Heavenly Father for His goodness in giving them an understanding of the Gospel, for making known to them that the hour of His judgments (upon Babylon) were at hand, and for making a way for their deliverance.[15]

Text from Latter-day Saint Hymnal *(1871), pp. 359–360; music from* Hymns *(Salt Lake City, 1948), 344.*
Other source: 12 Hafen 269.

14. *Ye Elders of Israel*

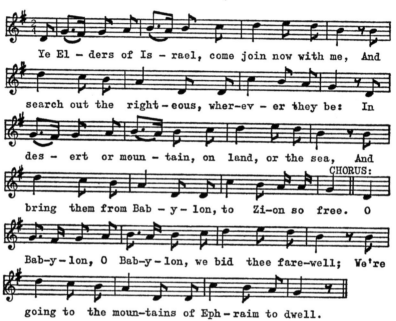

Ye Elders of Israel, come join now with me,
And search out the righteous, wherever they be;
In desert or mountain, on land, or the sea,
And bring them from Babylon to Zion so free.

Chorus:
O Babylon, O Babylon, we bid thee farewell;
We're going to the mountains of Ephraim to dwell.

[15] *Millennial Star*, April 11, 1857, p. 59.

The harvest is great and the lab'rers are few,
But if we're united, we all things can do;
We'll gather the wheat from the midst of the tares
And bring them from bondage, deep sorrows and snares.

We'll go to the poor, like our Captain of old,
And visit the weary, the hungry and cold;
We'll heal up their wounds, and we'll dry up their tears,
And lead them to Zion to dwell there for years.

We'll visit the feeble, the halt, dumb and blind,
And preach them the Gospel of Jesus so kind;
We'll cheer up their hearts with the news that he bore,
And point them to Zion for life evermore.

And when we have finished the work we've begun,
And the Priesthood in Zion shall say, "'Tis well done,"
With friends, wives and children, how happy we'll be,
And shout when the trumpet sounds, "Zion is free!"

15. *California*

To see the significance of this song and the two which follow, one needs to know the meaning of the term "Zion" as used in the Mormon Church. John Henry Evans explains the concept in *One Hundred Years of Mormonism:*

From the very beginning of the Church in this dispensation it seems there had been a peculiar charm for the Saints in the terms "Zion" and "New Jerusalem." To these their attention was first awakened, doubtless, by the *Book of Mormon.* For in this sacred volume they read that at some day future to the time when the book was written, a great and magnificent city, called the New Jerusalem, should be built somewhere on this continent, "unto the remnant of the seed of Joseph" and unto those "whose garments are white in the blood of the Lamb." And they were confirmed in this idea by revelations to the Prophet Joseph. As early as September, 1830, the Lord announced that "the City" should be built "on the borders by the Lamenites."[16]

As converts were made in our own country and elsewhere, they were advised to come to Zion (headquarters of the Church) and

[16] John Henry Evans, *One Hundred Years of Mormonism,* p. 139.

there participate in building the Kingdom of God. In *Hymns of the Latter-day Saints* (p. 81), is the song, "Israel, Israel, God is Calling," some words of which are, "Come to Zion, come to Zion, and within her walls rejoice." Basically this admonition and promise is the theme of these songs.

Elder John Parry, of Welsh descent, wrote this song in September, 1848, only a little over a year after the pioneer company settled in Salt Lake Valley; but already "Zion's Mount" was established, "a land of peace and liberty."

Text from the Millennial Star, *January 1, 1849, p. 15.*
Tune: "Salem."

On Zion's land there shall be rest
For all the Saints that's here oppress'd
On Zion's Mount we shall be free,
And there we'll have our jubilee.

Chorus:
To California's land we'll go,
Where, from the mountains, wine doth flow;
A land of peace and liberty,
To California, go with me.

No tyrant shall annoy us there,
We'll serve our King without a fear;
In truth we'll join with one accord,
To sing loud anthems to our Lord.

The everlasting hills we'll view,
And to England, bid adieu;
In California's hearty plains
We'll meet to learn celestial strains.

O! Lend your aid, ye morning wings,
And guard me safe through ocean springs,
That we may wait the Jubilee,
For on the Mount the feast will be.

A feast of wines upon the lees,
With fat and marrow, and with these
The Lord will comfort Zion's band,
Her wilderness the Elder's land.

And like the garden of the Lord
Her desert bloom and skill afford
Great joy, and gladness, love and peace;
A voice of praise shall never cease.

Rejoice ye ransom'd with the Lord,
You shall return with one accord,
To sing and shout on Zion's hill,
Where sighs nor sorrows never thrill.

Come then my friends, let us prepare,
To go and build a temple there;
A temple high above the hills,
Whom Jesus with his presence fills.

For on the Mount our king shall reign
Henceforth, for e'er, we'll praise his name:
Then let our lyres be all prepared,
To strike the sound of heavenly choir.

Hosannah to the King of kings;
He comes with healing in his wings;
He comes with pow'r on earth to reign,
All kings shall bow unto his name.

⟨⟩ 16. *Our Ain Mountain Hame* ⟨⟩

From the time of its inception the Mormon Church has been a proselyting church; missionaries have gone out and brought converts home. To the Mormons a new dispensation of the Gospel had come, and the new Zion was being established.

Mormon theologians have now determined that the word Zion is used in the Scriptures in various contexts with differences in meaning; it may mean a people as well as a place. In recent years Church leaders have not put emphasis on a Zion place. Rather they have said that Zion is wherever the pure in heart dwell; consequently they have built temples in other lands and have advised people to stay at home and build the Kingdom of God there.

The past emphasis on "gathering to Zion" and enthusiasm engendered through it, however, have brought thousands of converts from foreign lands to the gathering place of the Saints. Converts who arrived soon caught the spirit of love for their mountain home.

John Lyon was a folk poet from Ireland whose songs were sung in Salt Lake Valley long before the Civil War. With other songs of his, this song was published by his son David R. Lyon in 1923. It was sung first by the composer in Salt Lake City in 1855.

Text from David R. Lyon, Songs of a Pioneer, *p. 21.*

Come all ye feeling faithful Saints who've crossed the prairie drear,
And I'll tell you what you'll do for those who're coming out this year,
Lay up in store for them, worthy of your Godlike name,
And you'll have our leaders' blessings when the Saints come hame.

The lambokins in their innocence upon the mountain brow
Are less subject to devouring wolves than all good Saints are now,
Then stretch your welcome hand to your brethren who would claim
Our aid to help them onward, to our ain mountain hame.

The widows, and the fatherless, the old, and young together
Who've toiled 'midst hunger, heat, and cold, and sickness sore
    together,
With songs of praise will come, with the sick, the blind, and lame,
To find a place of succor in our ain mountain hame.

For o'er the waving prairie like an endless sheet of light,
The caravans are rolling with some thousands on their flight
From the rage of war and famine, and a guilty world's shame,
To find a place of safety in our ain mountain hame.

Soon Zion in her beauty will shine forth upon the world,
In glorious light and majesty, when freedom's flag's unfurled,
And kings and queens from 'far, who hearing of her fame,
Will come to see her glory in our ain mountain hame.

Then you, my friends, who built her up, in glory and renown,
Will each receive for your reward a never-fading crown;
And brighter wreaths of glory than the tongue of man can name,
When this earth is made celestial—our ain mountain hame.

⟡ 17. *Zion the Home of an Honest Man* ⟡

The Church publication in England, the *Millennial Star*, undoubtedly played an important part, through publishing items of import, in encouraging the Saints to go to Zion. This song was printed there after it had been sung to the tune of "The Englishman." The didactic message is abvious.

Text from the Millennial Star, *January 8, 1859, p. 41.*

> There's a land far away in the west,
> A place by God assigned
> 'Tis there the wearied saint can rest,
> Or a stranger safety find;
> For there the prophets have declared
> The house of God shall be,
> On mountain tops it shall be reared
> That all the world may see.
> 'Tis a favored country—deny it who can;
> And there is a home for an honest man.
>
> The law from Zion shall go forth,
> It long has been foretold,
> To teach the nations of the earth,
> And save a ruined world;
> And from Jerusalem shall go
> The word of God with might,
> That man may learn and live and grow
> In purity and light
> 'Tis a favored country—deny it who can;
> And there is a home for an honest man.

⟡ 18. *The Bull Whacker* ⟡

When the Mormons left Nauvoo, they had many horses and mules, but they learned in going from Nauvoo to Iowa that oxen were better adapted to the strenuous draft work of pulling wagons on the long trek. So they traded horses and mules for oxen, and thus "mule skinners" became "bull whackers."

A song of the War of 1812 was published in *The Dime Song Book* in 1859 as "Root, Hog, or Die." It was very popular, and parodies of it are numerous. One of these was "The Bull Whacker," which tells of an ox-team driver on the Denver line. The Mormon song is an adaptation of "The Bull Whacker." It is interesting that in changing the Denver song to a Salt Lake song, the Mormons changed a line from "You've got to whip and holler, swear, but never cry" to "You've got to whip and holler; if you swear it's on the sly." Yet they retained lines that show a belligerent attitude; if anyone steals an ox, they will maul him with an ox bow.

In trekking west and in colonizing the Great Basin, Brigham Young was both a spiritual and a practical leader. Somewhat like the Old Testament leaders, he was an exacting and hard disciplinarian under the religious code. Thus every man had to sustain himself and all were equal as hogs are equal. The concept that "God helps them that help themselves" worked out practically as "Root, hog, or die."

Sung by Jesse Jepsen, St. George, Utah, April 17, 1960.

Other sources: 43 Hubbard 295; 52 Laws B21; 67 Emrich; 69 Columbia Records.

18. *The Bull Whacker*

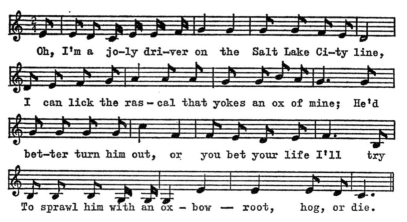

Oh, I'm a jolly driver on the Salt Lake City line,
I can lick the rascal that yokes an ox of mine;
He'd better turn him out, or you bet your life I'll try
To sprawl him with an ox-bow—root, hog, or die.

It's not so very pleasant when you start upon the road,
With an awkward team and a very heavy load.

You have to whip and holler; if you swear it's on the sly.
Go it if you like it, boys, root, hog, or die.

Out upon the road you have to go it as you can,
They won't try to please you or any other man.
You have to go it night and day, also wet and dry,
Go it if you like it, boys, root, hog, or die.

Out upon the road it is a very hard task,
The worst thing of all we have so long to fast.
Only have two meals a day, the third passes you by.
You eat jerked meat and like it—root, hog, or die.

Perhaps you'd like to know, boys, what we have to eat,
A small piece of bread but a smaller piece of meat,
A little fruit and beans, sugar on the sly.
Go it if you like it, boys, root, hog, or die.

Perhaps you'd like to know, boys, what we have to sup,
We have a little coffee and an old rusty cup.
A little of the Platte, a little alkali,
Big pig, little pig, root, hog, or die.

All day long you must be upon your feet,
You'll see "root, hog, or die" marked on every wagon seat.
The dust within your throat, the sand within your eye,
You'll get enough of that, boys, root, hog, or die.

Every day at noon we have something to do.
And if it's nothing else, we have an ox to shoe.
With our ropes we throw him down, and there we make him lie
While we tack the shoes on, root, hog, or die.

There is a fine sight to be seen upon the road,
The antelope and deer and the big sandy toad.
The elk and buffalo, the rabbits jump so high,
And the bloody redskins—root, hog, or die.

We arrived in Salt Lake City on the twenty-fourth of July[17]
The folks were all surprised for to see us in so soon.
We are jovial bull whackers on whom you can rely.
We're tough and can stand it, boys, root, hog, or die.

[17] The rhyme is broken here by the Mormon folk to give the correct date of the arrival of the Mormon pioneer company in Salt Lake Valley.

𝒢𝒦𝒮 19. *The Handcart Song* 𝒢𝒦𝒮

Few Mormon folksongs are as popular as this. Scarcely a record of Mormon songs has appeared without it. L. M. Hilton contributed it long ago to Austin Fife. Hilton, Sorrels, Clark, the Three D's, and others have sung it in hundreds of gatherings in Mormondom; children sing it in "Primary" (a Church auxiliary organization for children under twelve). The marching rhythm of the music gives zest and purpose to the foot-padding trek of handcart migration.

Of migrating west with handcarts, William E. Berrett says:

Most of the migrating Saints were outfitted with wagons drawn by horses or mules as a means of transporting food, clothing, and a few necessities. The cost of transporting emigrants from England to Salt Lake Valley rose so sharply in the early fifties that in 1856 a new experiment was tried to cut down the financial burden. Light two-wheeled carts made almost entirely of wood that could be pushed or pulled by hand were constructed for the purpose of hauling food, clothing, and bedding across the plains. The first emigrants to use handcarts came to America from England in 1856. These companies left Iowa City in the spring of that year and made the journey successfully, having walked and pushed or pulled their handcarts some twelve hundred miles. Two other handcart companies composed of British and Scandinavian Saints left Iowa City in late summer. . . . A premature winter descended upon them while they were still in Wyoming. Delays had already caused severe food shortages and bedding was insufficient for cold weather. Before help could reach them from Salt Lake Valley, Willie's Company of four hundred had buried seventy-five while Martin's Company of five hundred seventy-six had lost about one hundred fifty.

These tragedies lessened the use of the handcart and caused closer supervision of migrating companies.[18]

Davidson collected this song in 1945 from Dr. LeRoy Hafen and assigns authorship to William Hobbs. The Fifes have four versions in their collection, the earliest from L. M. Hilton in 1946.

Sung by L. M. Hilton, Ogden, Utah, July 18, 1959.

Other sources: 35 Davidson (1945); 39 Durham 21; 43 Hubbard 399; 44 Hubbard 122–123; 67 Emrich; 68 Fife MC I, 595 (L. M. Hilton, Ogden, Utah, 1946); three other entries in the Fife Collection; 69 Columbia Records; 70 Hilton; 71 Sorrels and Fife.

Ye saints who dwell on Europe's shore
Prepare yourselves for many more,

[18] William E. Berrett, *Doctrines of the Restored Church*, p. 68.

19. *The Handcart Song*

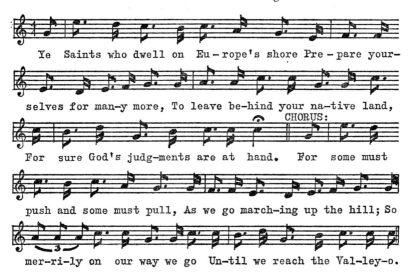

Ye Saints who dwell on Eu – rope's shore Pre – pare yourselves for man-y more, To leave be-hind your na–tive land,
For sure God's judg-ments are at hand. For some must
push and some must pull, As we go march-ing up the hill; So
mer-ri-ly on our way we go Un-til we reach the Val-ley-o.

CHORUS:

To leave behind your native land,
For sure God's judgments are at hand.
For you must cross the raging main
Before the promised land you gain
And with the faithful make a start
To cross the plains with your handcart.

Chorus:
For some must push and some must pull
As we go marching up the hill;
So merrily on our way we go
Until we reach the Valley-o.

The lands that boast of modern light
We know are all as dark as night
Where poor men toil and want for bread,
Where peasant folks are blindly led.
These lands that boast of liberty
You ne'er again will wish to see
When you from Europe make a start
To cross the plains with your handcart.

As on the road the carts are pulled
'Twould very much surprise the world
To see the old and feeble dame
Thus lend a hand to pull the same.
And maidens fair will dance and sing,
Young men more happy than a king,
And children will laugh and play
Their strength increasing day by day.

And long before the Valley's gained,
We will be met upon the plain
With music sweet and friends so dear
And fresh supplies our hearts to cheer.
And then with music and with song
How cheerfully we'll march along
And thank the day we made a start
To cross the plains in our handcart.

When you get there among the rest,
Obedient be and you'll be blessed
And in God's chambers be shut in
While judgments cleanse the earth from sin,
For we do know it will be so,
God's servants spoke it long ago,
We say it is high time to start
To cross the plains with your handcart.

20. *The Handcart Song (Missionary)*

In 1857 seventy-six missionaries were called to go on missions. The group went from Salt Lake City to Florence, Nebraska, pushing handcarts. On the first night out one of their number, Phillip Margetts, wrote this song. It was sung en route.

Text from the Millennial Star, *August 15, 1857.*
Other sources: 12 Hafen 275; 35 Davidson 280.
Tune: "Oh, Susannah."

No purse no script, they bear with them, but cheerfully
  they start
And cross the plains a thousand miles, and draw with them
  a cart
Ye nations list! The men of God, from Zion now they come,
Clothed with the Priesthood and the Power, they gather
  Israel home!

Chorus:
Then cheer up ye Elders, you to the world will show,
That Israel must be gathered soon, their oxen are too slow.

Ye pious men whose sympathy is touched for fallen man,
A pattern now is set for you, just beat it if you can;
Here's men who're called to go abroad the Gospel to impart
They leave their friends and homes so dear and start with
  their handcart.

Now competition is the rage throughout the world, 'tis true,
To head the Mormons they must rise far earlier than they do,
For Mormonism it is sound, without a crack or flaw,
They know the arts and sciences, and we're learning how to
  draw.

Some folks would ask, Why do you start with carts, come
  tell I pray?
We answer: When our Prophet speaks, the Elders all obey;
Since Brigham has the way laid out that's best for us,
  we'll try,
Stand off ye sympathetic fools, the handcarts now or die.

Then come ye faithful ministers, with blessings now we'll go
To gather out the honest hearts from darkness and from woe;
Our strength increasing day by day as from this land we part,
We'll bless the day that we were called to go with our
  handcart.

21. *The Upper California*

The "Upper California" referred to here contained nearly all the country in western United States on the mainland west of the Rocky Mountains. This song was composed by John Taylor, who later became third president of the Church, and was sung by the Saints as they trekked across the plains. Like many other songs, it is one which was designed to give them courage to go forward and hope for prosperity and happiness at journey's end.

Sung by Robert Christmas, Provo, Utah, January, 1960.
Other sources: 35 Davidson 282; 39 Durham 306.

21. *The Upper California*

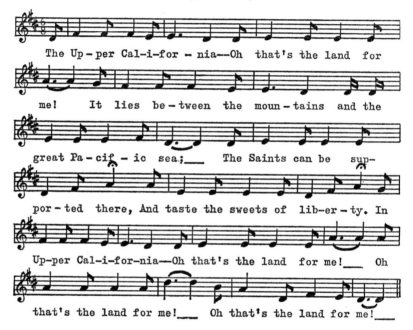

The Up-per Cal-i-for - nia—Oh that's the land for
me! It lies be-tween the moun - tains and the
great Pa - cif - ic sea;___ The Saints can be sup-
por - ted there, And taste the sweets of lib-er - ty. In
Up-per Cal-i-for-nia—Oh that's the land for me!___ Oh
that's the land for me!___ Oh that's the land for me!___

The Upper California—Oh, that's the land for me!
It lies between the mountains and the great Pacific sea;
The Saints can be supported there,
And taste the sweets of liberty.
In Upper California—Oh, that's the land for me!
Oh that's the land for me! Oh that's the land for me!

We'll go and lift our standard, we'll go there and be free;
We'll go to California and have our jubilee;
A land that blooms with endless spring,
A land of life and liberty,
With flocks and herds abounding—Oh, that's the land for me!

We'll burst off all our fetters and break the Gentile yoke,
For long it has beset us, but now it shall be broke;
No more shall Jacob bow his neck;
Henceforth he shall be great and free
In Upper California—Oh, that's the land for me!

We'll reign, we'll rule and triumph, and God shall be our King;
The plains, the hills and valleys shall with hosannas ring;
Our towers and temples there shall rise
Along the great Pacific sea,
In Upper California—Oh, that's the land for me!

Then join with me, my brethren, and let us hasten there;
We'll lift our glorious standard and raise our house of prayer;
We'll call on all nations around
To join our standard and be free
In Upper California—Oh, that's the land for me!

22. This Is the Place

or

Brigham Young, The Western Pioneer

The phrase "This is the place" has become a legend in Utah. The folk believe that Brigham Young had seen in vision the valley where the Saints were to settle. When his wagon emerged from the canyon to a position where the valley could be viewed and he "raised upon his elbow and said 'This is the place,' " he spoke as a prophet. Now, newspapers, advertisements, and chambers-of-commerce blurbs repeatedly use the phrase, and monuments memorialize it for future generations.

This song, composed by Myron Crandall in the 1930's, is a favorite for pioneer celebrations.

Sung by Robert Christmas, Provo, Utah, January, 1960.
Text from Fife, Saints of Sage and Saddle, p. 327.
*Other sources: 68 Fife MC I, 565 (Myron Crandall, Ogden, 1946);
69 Columbia Records.*

22. *This Is the Place*

or

Brigham Young, the Western Pioneer

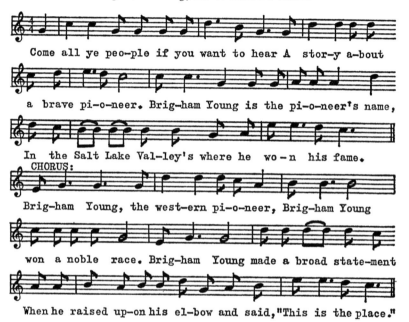

Come all ye peo-ple if you want to hear A stor-y a-bout

a brave pi-o-neer. Brig-ham Young is the pi-o-neer's name,

In the Salt Lake Val-ley's where he wo-n his fame.

CHORUS:

Brig-ham Young, the west-ern pi-o-neer, Brig-ham Young

won a noble race. Brig-ham Young made a broad state-ment

When he raised up-on his el-bow and said,"This is the place."

Come all ye people if you want to hear
A story about a brave pioneer.
Brigham Young is the pioneer's name,
In the Salt Lake Valley's where he won his fame.
He told his people on the Mississippi River,
"You better get ready, we are leaving forever.
We'll turn our faces out to the West,
Do not get discouraged for we'll do our best."

Chorus:
Brigham Young, the western pioneer,
Brigham Young won a noble race.
Brigham Young made a broad statement
When he raised upon his elbow and said, "This is the place."

From Germany and Holland, Denmark, Sweden, France and
    Wales,
Johnny Bull and Scotch and Irish with their clever Irish tales,
He put them in a melting pot—I give him many thanks,
When he stirred 'em up a little bit they all were Yanks.
He says, "Repair your wagons, your carriages and carts,
Shoe your horses, mules and oxen, we are about to start.
Make roads through the valleys and bridges o'er the rivers,"
And they had to travel slow because they never had a flivver.

They reached Salt Lake Valley on July the twenty-fourth,
A thousand miles they traveled—they were very tired, of
    course.
Their leader was sick, weariness was on his face,
But he raised upon his elbow and said, "This is the place."
Some went to California, they wouldn't heed advice,
They didn't seem to prosper, were as poor as church mice.
Some joined the other churches and I have a little hunch
They wished the heck they'd never quit the Brigham Young
    bunch.

They met old Jim Bridger in the country of Wyoming,
He would give a thousand dollars for an ear of corn a-growing.
They instituted irrigation, had fine crops,
'Till along came the crickets and the old grass-hops.
The crickets and the grasshoppers, they got so awful bad
The saints tried to kill 'em, they fought 'til they were mad.
The Lord sent the sea gulls, in about two shakes
How they heaved them over in the Great Salt Lake!

Before they left the Middle-West a message came from Uncle
    Sam:
"We want five hundred volunteers to fight the Mexican!"
"We're loyal to the Stars and Stripes, want everyone to know
If we haven't got five hundred men our women they will go."
The old stage coach, the Pony Express

Carried mail and passengers from East to the West.
They moved the best they could before the days of rail
Along the Emigrant Road and the Oregon Trail.

They built wagon roads and railroads and irrigation ditches,
Woolen mills to manufacture dresses and breeches,
They dug for gold and silver and a little copper, too,
And soon they were better off than back in Nauvoo.
Forty years a-building a Temple in Salt Lake,
Another one in Manti, one in the Logan Stake,
Another down in Dixie—now there's eight all told
And we all work diligently, young and old.

Once they had a celebration up in old Cottonwood,
They were happy and doing the very best they could
Hard news came to Brigham, Johnston's Army on the wing,
"Before we let them enter we'll destroy everything!"
He built Salt Lake Theatre, erected many schools
To educate the kiddies 'cause they wanted no fools.
He called 'em his busy bees, they built a lot of hives,
And he ought to go to Heaven with his nineteen wives.

     23. *This Is the Place*

Sung by L. M. Hilton, Ogden, Utah, January, 1960.
Tune: "Nay, Speak No Ill," a Mormon hymn.

> "This is the place for the Temple Square"
> Said Brigham Young to his council there.
> He struck the ground a sounding blow
> With his cane so the world might know.
> "We'll build a house of God," said he,
> "That all the world will come and see;
> Mankind will yet regard with praise
> These Mormon Saints of latter-days."
>
> "This is the place," the surveyors said,
> Leveling their instruments ahead;
> The site for the Temple then they planned out
> Mid the sagebrush on desert land.

The ox-team excavators came
And excavated their way to fame,
While forty men sought distant hills
With ox-team sleds and granite drills.
"This is the place," the drivers said,
Urging their plodding beasts ahead.
With giant blocks of stone each day
Was how the walls were built to stay.
Up, up to towering heights they grew
'Till towers themselves rose into view,
And bronzed Moroni showed on high
With trumpet raised to the azure sky.

"This is the place," the speaker said,
"Where Brigham Young himself was led
By God's hand, to here create
This Temple which we dedicate,
For forty years of toil have passed,
The Temple finished here at last
To stand till Gabriel's trumpet sounds
And peace for all on earth abounds."

"This is the place in all the west."
Its claims the traveling stranger guessed
Where Brigham Young and his Mormon band
First built in Utah's wonderland.
And so t'will be year after year,
They'll criticize or praise and cheer.
When we have long since quit the race
Will still be heard, "This is the place."

24. Sego Lily

Sentimental and elementary in tone, "Sego Lily" is sung more by
children than by adults in Utah. The simple melody and saccharine
words may not touch one's emotions unless they lie exposed. L. M.
Hilton, speaking in harmony with the prevalent tone of the song,
said: "The sego lily is the only thing that lifted up its head to wel-

come the pioneers when they came to Salt Lake Valley." Perhaps that is the reason it was chosen the Utah state flower.

Sung by L. M. Hilton, Ogden, Utah, July 18, 1959.
Other source: 70 Hilton.

Greetings to thee, Sego Lily,
Blossom of the sagebrush desert
Lending us thy blessing dear.

Tell me, Sego, of thy story,
When thou did first grace these hills,
Whose eyes were the first to see you,
Who the first to know thy thrills?

When God's all-creating power
Placed thee here in the desert fair,
Was the first sego lily as perfect
As thou art now nestled there?

Did you suffer and overcome hardship
When you came to this region so drear,
Did God send you, dear little flower,
To Utah as a pioneer?

Did you feel a glow of pleasure
When the pioneer arrived
And your roots supplied their hunger
As the food till they revived?

One more question, Sego Lily,
Answer this my last request,
Wilt thou be there with the angels
Should I chance to join the blest?

24. *Sego Lily*

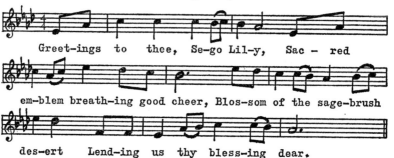

Greet-ings to thee, Se-go Lil-y, Sac - red em-blem breath-ing good cheer, Blos-som of the sage-brush des-ert Lend-ing us thy bless-ing dear.

25. *The Campfire Meeting*

or

Gather Round the Campfire, Brethren

When the pioneer Saints arrived in the Great Basin, they named the provisional state Deseret, a name taken from the *Book of Mormon* meaning "beehive"—a symbol of industry. Although the name "Deseret" was replaced by "Utah" when statehood was granted, the word "Deseret" is used profusely within the state and Church in such names as Deseret Sunday School Union, Deseret Industries, *Deseret News*, Deseret Detection Agency, Deseret Travel Agency, and Deseret Federal Savings and Loan, and the symbolic beehive is seen on various documents throughout the Church.

The song refers to the unfurling of the Gospel banner in the state of Deseret.

Sung by L. M. Hilton, Ogden, Utah, July 18, 1959.

25. *The Campfire Meeting*

or

Gather Round the Campfire, Brethren

Gath-er round the camp-fire, breth-ren, On these plains we here have met To re-joice and thank the God of Hea-ven For the State of Des-er-et.

Gather round the campfire, brethren,
On these plains we here have met
To rejoice and thank the God of Heaven
For the State of Deseret.

Chorus:
We can build our homes in safety
Where these mountain bulwarks stand;

We can serve our Lord and here be happy
In this sacred, promised land.

Deseret in all her splendor
Will one day attract the world;
Modern Israel's glorious gospel banner
To all men will be unfurled.

ᏜᎯᏜ 26. *The Seagulls and the Crickets* ᏜᎯᏜ

The never-to-be-forgotten incident related in this song occurred, according to tradition, in the summer of 1848.[19] Two thousand people had gathered into Salt Lake Valley by the fall of 1847. There had been no harvest. Before winter was over, vegetables and fruits were completely exhausted; flour brought from Winter Quarters had nearly all been consumed, and meat was scarce.

In the fall the colonizers planted nearly 2,000 acres of winter wheat, in the spring about 3,000 acres more. Excellent germination and growth cheered the people to hope for a bounteous harvest.

But they had not thought of the menace of crickets. They had only been amused when they watched Indians gather insects for winter food. Now the loathesome, black, inch-and-a-half-long pests swept down in clouds from the hillsides like a sea of black, turning and blending the green fields to gray.

A battle was waged with men, women, and children against crickets. Frantically the people beat and flayed the pests into ditches, buried them in trenches, drove them into fires. Then when their puny hands could no longer withstand the relentless push of the insects, in sweaty exhaustion and despairing defeat they resorted to the only alternative—prayer.

Then exploring seagulls discovered a food supply. Soon the gray-white birds descended on the grain fields, not to eat the grain but to devour the devourers. They came in thousands to eat and gorge, to gorge, vomit, and eat again. Thus the famine was averted; the pioneers were saved.

This is the legend, so deeply ingrained in the Mormon folk, as it is told in Sunday School to children and as it continues to live. His-

---

[19] For verification of the date and history of this event, see Roberts, *A Comprehensive History of the Church*, III, 331–334.

torian Lyman S. Tyler and others have observed that early diaries often mention the menace of crickets but do not tell of the seagulls coming to eat the crickets.

Sung by L. M. Hilton, Ogden, Utah, July 18, 1959.
Other sources: 42 Fife 322; 69 Columbia Records; 70 Hilton; 71 Sorrels and Fife.

26. *The Seagulls and the Crickets*

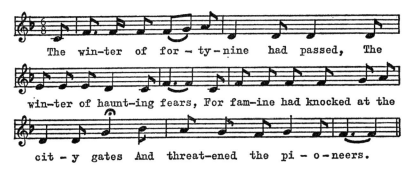

The win-ter of for - ty - nine had passed, The win-ter of haunt-ing fears, For fam-ine had knocked at the cit - y gates And threat-ened the pi - o - neers.

The winter of forty-nine had passed,[20]
The winter of haunting fears,
For famine had knocked at the city gates
And threatened the pioneers.
But spring with its smiling skies lent grace
And cheer to the hosts within
And they tilled their fields with a new born trust
And the courage to fight and win.

With a thrill of life the tender shoots
Burst forth from the virgin plain,
And each day added its ray of hope
For a blessing of ripened grain.
But lo, in the east strange clouds appeared
And dark became the sun
And down from the mountain sides there swept
A scourge that the boldest shun.

---

[20] The discrepancy in the date given here and that in the introductory material above shows folk inaccuracy.

Black crickets by tens of millions came
Like fog on the British coast,
And the finger of devastation marked
Its course on the Mormon host.
With a vigor that desperation fanned
They battled and smote and slew,
But the clouds still gathered and broke afresh
Till the fields that waved were few.

With visions of famine and want and woe
They prayed from hearts sincere
When lo, from the west came other clouds
To succor the pioneers.
'Twas seagulls feathered in angel white,
And angels they were forsooth.
The seagulls there by the thousands came
To battle in very truth.

They charged down upon the cricket hordes
And gorging them day and night
They routed the devastating hosts
And the crickets were put to flight.
And heads were bowed as they thanked their God
And they reaped while the devil raved.
The harvest was garnered to songs of praise
And the pioneers were saved.

 27. *Is the Story True?*

Sung by L. M. Hilton, Ogden, Utah, October, 1959.

"Seagull, gentle Seagull,
Soaring in the blue,
Stop and tell me really
Is the story true?
Were you sent by heaven
In our hour of dread
To eat up the crickets
And save the children's bread?"

27. *Is the Story True?*

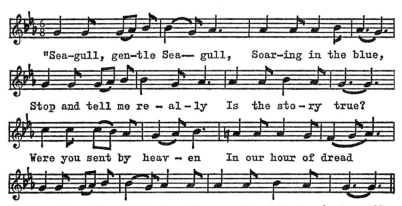

"Sea-gull, gen-tle Sea— gull, Soar-ing in the blue,

Stop and tell me re - al - ly Is the sto - ry true?

Were you sent by heav - en In our hour of dread

To eat up the crick-ets And save the chil-dren's bread?"

"Yes, dear little children,
What you say is true,
We were sent by heaven
To save the grain for you.
We filled up on crickets
Disgorged and ate again,
Thus your prayers were answered
For we saved the grain."

"Seagull, gentle Seagull,
Soaring in the blue,
Now I know that really
That sweet story's true.
You were sent by heaven
In our hour of dread
To eat up the crickets
And save the children's bread."

28. *In Defense of Polygamy*

Joseph Smith, the Prophet, instituted polygamy[21] in the Church before his death; in fact, plural marriage and teaching led to his martyrdom. Accepted as a command from God, "celestial marriage," as it was called, was supported by subsequent leaders of the Church. Brigham Young, after bringing the Saints to Utah, said in an inappropriate metaphor, "We must gird up our loins and fulfill this, just as we would any other duty."[22] Mormons did accept the practice as a duty, made mandatory by revelation from God. This song and the two following reflect loyalty to the "Principle," and hostility and vindictiveness toward enemies.

The time of the origin of this song is about 1890, the year Wilford Woodruff, President of the Mormon Church, issued a document, approved by the Church, officially prohibiting polygamy. This manifesto came after extended efforts on the part of the federal government to eliminate the practice.

Text from William H. Avery, Blackfoot, Idaho, 1933.

Sung by Dean Farnsworth, Provo, Utah, May 24, 1959, using the music as I remembered it from Mr. Avery's singing.

Other sources: 26 Cheney 133 (1936); 43 Hubbard 456; 68 Fife MC I, 704 (Effie and Bess Snow, St. George, Utah, 1947).

> There is a bunch of whiskey bloats perluding[23] our fair land;
> They are here to see our country laws enforced;
> They say that the laws, there ain't enough to punish Mormon
>   crime,
> And for more, they are always on the yelp.
>
> They say that if the Mormons will polygamy deny,
> Like themselves take to houses of ill fame,
> They will call them friends and brethren and will take them
>   by the hand;
> But in this, I think, they'll find they are lame.

---

[21] The precise term would be *polygyny*. *Polygamy*, however, is the common term used by Mormons and non-Mormons alike in referring to the Mormon practice. For that reason I shall use it in this work.

[22] Franklyn D. Richards, ed., *Brigham Young's Discourses*, II, 266.

[23] Folk corruption of "polluting."

28. *In Defense of Polygamy*

There is a bunch of whis-key bloats per-lud-ing our fair
land; They are here to see our coun-try laws en-forced;
They say that the laws, there ain't e-nough to pun-ish
Mor-mon crime, And for more, they are al-ways on the yelp.

CHORUS:
Mur-ry holds the reins; the whip be-longs to Zane; Old
Ire-land and his aid will go be-low; And old Dix-on
will do well to en-gage a case in Hell, For the
road he is on will take him there, I know.

Chorus:
Murry holds the reins; the whip belongs to Zane;
Old Ireland and his aid will go below;
And old Dixon will do well to engage a case in Hell,
For the road he is on will take him there, I know.

They say that the Mormons are a set of low-down dragons,
And they're going to rid the land of such a crew,
Or they will build pens large enough to hold Mormon men;
And in them they will shove the women, too.

29. *Put You into Limbo*

Of this song Austin Fife says: "The deputies sent by the federal government to apprehend and incarcerate polygamists encountered vigorous resistance. This song is one of the many that tell of their plight. A whole generation of little Mormons played as 'deps and cohabs' instead of 'Indians and cowboys.' "

Text and introduction from Fife, Saints of Sage and Saddle, *p. 332. Other sources: cf. 43 Hubbard 418; 68 Fife MC I, 706 (Francis Y. Morse, St. George, Utah, 1947).*

Now you co-habs still dodging 'round, you'd better keep on
  underground,
For if with Number Two you're found, they'll put you into
  limbo.

Some gents will meet you at the gate, and with complexion,
  height and weight,
The contents of your pockets take, when you get into limbo.

They'll shave your face and mow your hair and give you striped
  clothes to wear,
And see that you have the best of fare, when you get into limbo.

Oh, when you pass the double door . . .[24] within begin to roar,
As fish, fresh fish, is all the go, when you get into limbo.

And if you do not fall in line, they'll put you into fifty-nine,
And take away your copper tine, when you get into limbo.

Oh, here you'll find both men and boys making different kinds
  of toys,
Bridles, whips and walking sticks, when you get into limbo.

[24] Imperfect recording.

ᏯᎤᎩ 30. *Ever Constant* ᏯᎤᎩ

During the period in which the Church sanctioned the practice of plurality of wives, many Mormon men who had more than one wife were imprisoned by federal authorities. The song following is a letter of an unknown Mormon wife written to her imprisoned husband.

Sung by L. M. Hilton, Ogden, Utah, October, 1959.
Tune: "A Poor Wayfaring Man of Grief."

> The dear ones now have all been scattered
> From the homes where once we dwelled,
> And though the chamber now is vacant
> Where of old in prayers we knelt,
> And though I seldom see the faces
> That would greet me there with thee,
> Still my own heart and prayers unchanging
> Meet and center all in thee.
>
> *Chorus:*
> Oh yes, my love, still ever constant
> To my vows and thee I'll be,
> And though thy presence is denied me,
> Heart and soul I'm true to thee.
>
> Ye know the dungeon walls surround you
> Who has claimed me for your own,
> And though they falsely may accuse you,
> Still I love but you alone.
> Though for your sake I may not own you,
> May not even bear your name,
> Yet in my heart my thoughts and prayers
> You'll be my own, dear, still the same.
>
> They need not think that true affection
> Can be crushed by cruel deeds,
> Or that long or constant separation
> Can turn false the heart that bleeds.
> A woman's love will never perish
> While the heart she loves is true;
> An eternal stream, her love it floweth
> Ever constant, ever true.

☙ 31. *Doo Dah* ☙

This song and the three following may be called antifederalist songs. When the state of Deseret was admitted as a territory in 1850, President Fillmore appointed Brigham Young as governor and non-Mormons to many official posts. Conflicts arose between Mormons and federal officials. A government-appointed Federal Judge, William W. Drummond, who had come to Utah in 1855, was hated by the Mormons for his "drunkenness and immoral conduct." When his licentious living was disclosed, he left the territory. In his report to the government he charged the Mormons with refusal to obey civil law, with perpetration of a secret murder organization, with destruction of court records, and with discrimination in the administration of the law. Others of like mind confirmed these charges.[25]

Motivated by these reports and by political expediency, President Buchanan sent Johnston's Army to Utah to enforce Mormon submission. Considering these charges false, the Mormons did not peaceably submit. Brigham Young organized for defense and declared that God would come to his peoples' aid.

The author of this song, Isaac B. Nash, recorded in his journal:

On July 24, 1857, a party was given by President Young at Big Cottonwood Canyon and a great many were present. While we were there, the news was brought into camp by Porter Rockwell and Jud Stoddard that General Joe [Albert Sidney] Johnston had started with a part of the United States Army for Utah to take our leaders prisoners and drive us from our homes. At this time I wrote the song "Doo Dah" and sang it afterward in the tabernacle.

Text copied from Isaac B. Nash's journal, in possession of his great-great granddaughter, Carma Sandberg.
Sung by L. M. Hilton, Ogden, Utah, July 18, 1959.
Other Sources: 22 Stenhouse 370; 43 Hubbard 442.

> Come brethren listen to my song,
>   Doo-dah, doo-dah,
> I don't intend to keep you long,
>   Doo-dah, doo-dah day.
> 'Bout Uncle Sam I'm going to sing,

[25] See John Henry Evans, *One Hundred Years of Mormonism*, pp. 463–465.

31. *Doo Dah*

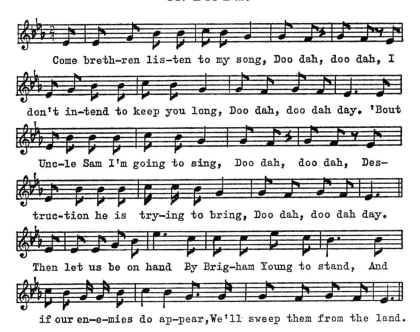

Come breth-ren lis-ten to my song, Doo dah, doo dah, I

don't in-tend to keep you long, Doo dah, doo dah day. 'Bout

Unc-le Sam I'm going to sing, Doo dah, doo dah, Des-

truc-tion he is try-ing to bring, Doo dah, doo dah day.

Then let us be on hand By Brig-ham Young to stand, And

if our en-e-mies do ap-pear, We'll sweep them from the land.

> Doo-dah, doo-dah,
> Destruction he is trying to bring
> Doo-dah, doo-dah day.

Chorus:
> Then let us be on hand
> By Brigham Young to stand,
> And if our enemies do appear,
> We'll sweep them from the land.

> Johnston's Army's on the way,
> The Mormon people for to slay,
> And if he comes we'll have some fun,
> To see him and his "Jinnies" run.

> Johnston's Army's in a sweat,
> He swears the Mormons he'll upset,
> But the Mormon people all are one,
> United in the Gospel plan.

There's seven hundred wagons on the way,
Their cattle are numerous too they say,
To let them perish 'twould be a sin,
So we'll take all they have for bringing them in.

So here's long life to Brigham Young,
And Heber too, for they are one;
May they and Daniel live to see
This people gain their liberty.

Individual accounts of details related to the coming of the army to Salt Lake Valley differ. Clarissa Young Spencer says that the people assumed that the coming army would be under command of the Indian fighter, General Harney, and that Brother Poulter composed a song containing the lines,

Squaw Killer Harney's on his way
The Mormon people for to slay.[26]

Two stanzas, powerful in use of snarl words, with these lines and others are given by Davidson in "Mormon Songs," *Journal of American Folklore*, LVIII (October–December, 1945), 256.

Old Sam has sent, I understand,
A Missouri ass to rule our land,
But if he comes we'll have some fun,
To see him and his juries run.

Old Squaw-Killer Harney is on his way,
The Mormon People for to slay.
Now, if he comes, the truth I'll tell,
Our boys will drive him down to hell.

❧ 32. *If Uncle Sam's Determined* ❧

Brigham Young and the Mormon people decided that they would not leave homes, farms, and businesses to invaders as they had in Nauvoo, Illinois. They would leave a scorched earth if enemies attempted to possess the city.

When it finally became evident that despite opposition the army would come into the Valley, thirty thousand people packed a few belongings into covered wagons and started south. Some daring

---

[26] Clarissa Young Spencer and Mable Harmon, *One Who Was Valiant*, p. 84.

young men were commissioned by Brigham Young to burn the city
if the troops attempted to enter. My grandfather, Shepherd Pierce
Hutchings, was one of these young men. Fortunately, the city was
not burned. The army passed by and camped about forty miles to
the south.

The resolution of the Mormons to burn the city is expressed in
this song.

*Text from Davidson, "Mormon Songs," Journal of American
Folklore, LVIII (October–December, 1945), 287, quoted from Nels
Anderson, Deseret Saints (Chicago, 1942), p. 170.*

> If Uncle Sam's determined
>   On his very foolish plan,
> The Lord will fight our battles
>   And we'll help Him if we can.
>
> If what they now propose to do
>   Should ever come to pass,
> We'll burn up every inch of wood
>   And every blade of grass.
>
> We'll throw down all our houses,
>   Every soul shall emigrate.
> And we'll organize ourselves
>   Into a roving mountain state.

33. *Johnston's Army Episode*

On September 15, 1857, after it appeared certain that the United
States Army would enter Mormon country, Brigham Young, acting
as governor (though he knew he was to be replaced), proclaimed the
territory under martial law and forbade armed forces to enter. The
Mormon militia, the Nauvoo Legion, then in Salt Lake Valley, con-
sisted of over six thousand men. It had originated in Nauvoo with
Joseph Smith as commander; in Utah, General Daniel H. Wells was
in command.

On September 29 General Wells left Salt Lake City for Echo
Canyon where he established headquarters for 1,250 men. In prepa-
ration for resisting the oncoming Johnston's Army, these soldiers

dug trenches across the canyon, threw up breastworks, and loosened rocks on heights.

The war actually amounted to the establishment by Mormons of fortifications in canyon approaches to prevent the army from entering the Valley and of organized harassment of the approaching army by a small and fearless group of Mormon boys under the direction of Lot Smith. This action forced Johnston's Army to spend the winter in improvised shelters on Black's Fork.

Happily no blood was shed. Through the intercession of a good friend of the Mormons, Colonel Thomas L. Kane, a peace commission was set up which led to arbitration.

This song was composed by militia men. The text is from a journal kept by Shepherd Pierce Hutchings, my grandfather, and preserved by my mother, Eliza M. Hutchings Cheney. The tune is Yankee Doodle, the most parodied of all military songs.
Other sources: 35 Davidson 286; 44 Hubbard 125.

When Uncle Sam he first set out his army to destroy us
Says he, "The Mormons we will route, they will no more annoy
    us."
The force he sent was competent to "try" and "hang" for treason,
That is, I mean it would have been, but don't you know the
    reason?

As they were going up the Platte singing many a lusty ditty,
Saying we'll do this and we'll do that when we get to Salt Lake
    City.
And sure enough, when they got there, they made the Mormons
    stir, Sir.
That is, I mean they would have done, but, oh, they didn't get
    there.

Chorus:
There's great commotion in the East about the Mormon question,
The problem is, to say the least, too much for their digestion.

When they got within two hundred miles, the old boys they were
    saying,
"We'll put an end to Mormon crime: we'll catch them while
    they're sleeping,

We'll hang each man that has two wives, we've plenty of rope
quite handy."
That is, I mean they would have had, but Smith burned it on
"Sandy."

Then they returned with awful tales, saying the Mormons beat
the devil;
They ride up hill and over rock as fast as on the level.
And if perchance you shoot one down, and surely think he's
dead, Sir;
The first you know he's on his horse, and pushing on ahead, Sir.

Then on Hanis Fork they camped awhile, saying, "We'll wait a
little longer.
'Til Johnston and his men come up and make us a little stronger.
Then we'll go on, take Brigham Young, and Heber and his
companion."
That is, I mean they would have done, but were afraid of Echo
Canyon.

Now Uncle Sam, take my advice, you'd better stay at home, Sir!
You need your money and your men to defend your rights at
home, Sir!
But if perchance you need some help, the Mormons will be yours,
Sir!
They've helped you once and will again, that is, if they've a
mind, Sir.

෧ 34. *Strong Is the Power of Brigham's God* ෧

His army having been harassed by General Wells' Legion from
September 29 until winter snows came, General Johnston decided
not to try a winter campaign. When news of his decision reached
Salt Lake City, Brigham Young called the greater part of the Legion
home, leaving only fifty men to guard the pass in Echo Canyon. To
celebrate their return, Eliza R. Snow composed this song.

Text contributed by Jay Healey, Provo, Utah, March, 1961.
Collected from Jenny Hancock, Provo, Utah.

> Strong is the power of Brigham's God,
> His name is a terror to our foes,
> Ye were a barrier strong and broad
> As our high mountains crowned with snows.
> Then welcome, sons of light and truth,
> Heroes in both age and youth.

35. *The United Order*

"In the first two decades following the arrival of the Saints in Utah, several attempts were made to implement the 'United Order,' a theocratic social system in which goods and facilities were owned and used in common. Orderville was one of the most successful of these colonies."

Introduction, music, and text from Fife, Saints of Sage and Saddle, *p. 325. Fife MC 1, 695 (Mrs. Elvira Cox Blackburn, Orderville, Utah, 1947).*
Other source: 43 Hubbard 396.

35. *The United Order*

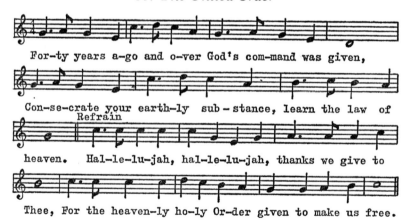

For-ty years a-go and o-ver God's com-mand was given,

Con-se-crate your earth-ly sub-stance, learn the law of

Refrain

heaven. Hal-le-lu-jah, hal-le-lu-jah, thanks we give to

Thee, For the heaven-ly ho-ly Or-der given to make us free.

Forty years ago and over God's command was given,
Consecrate your earthly substance, learn the law of heaven.

Chorus:
Hallelujah, hallelujah, thanks we give to Thee,
For the heavenly holy Order given to make us free.

Unite together, join the Order, is the call today,
Let us all with hearts rejoicing say we will obey.

Live together, work together, angels do above;
Each one try to help the other, this will bring true love.

Be ye one in earthly blessings, no distinction found,
Bless the widow, help the aged, as one family bound.

We're a little band of workers striving with our might
To obey the prophet Brigham for we know 'tis right.

Give us strength, eternal Father, wisdom too we pray,
For we are as little children learning day by day.

Men may mock and make derision, Satan too may rail,
But our motto must be, "Onward! Never, never fail."

Now again the Lord has spoken, hear the prophet's voice,
Let us all with hearts and voices say we will rejoice.

Here we dedicate, Our Father, wives and children dear,
Thou wilt help us and sustain us if we persevere.

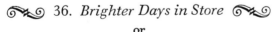

36. *Brighter Days in Store*
or
Brigham's Hard Times Come Again No More

Unlike the Stephen Foster song, "Hard Times Come Again No More," this song as Mormon folk sing it is not doleful; rather the words "brighter days in store" are amplified by the fast tempo and joyful tone. It was especially well done in this respect by the sixteen-voice choir who sang it for Columbia Records' Mormon Legacy recording.

Sung by L. M. Hilton, Ogden, Utah, July 18, 1959.

Other sources: 42 Fife 85; 68 Fife MC I, 572 (L. M. Hilton, Ogden, 1946); two other listings in the Fife Collection; 69 Columbia Records; 71 Sorrels and Fife.

I will sing of the Mormons, the people of the Lord,
Since the time that Joseph prayed for light,
And the way they've been guided by Jesus' holy light
And saved by power of his might.

Chorus:
'Tis the song, the sigh of the Mormons,
Hard times, hard times long have pressed us sore;
Many days they have lingered around our cabin door,
But now we've brighter days in store.

Each time that the wicked have tried to overthrow
And to bring the work of God to naught,
The way has been opened for the Saints of God to escape,
A ram in the thicket was caught.

The grasshoppers, crickets, and mobbers all combined
Were powerless to crush our noble cause.
The more we are hated, the more we are maligned,
The more the church of Jesus grows.

☞ 37. *The Utah Iron Horse* ☜

After twenty-one years of hardship in transporting converts to the Salt Lake Valley via ox team, wagon trains, and handcarts, Brigham Young welcomed the coming of the first transcontinental railroad. Clarissa Young Spencer, daughter of Brigham Young, gave the following account:

Each change and advance in methods of communication and transportation brought this inland empire into closer touch with the rest of the world until the brightest dreams and hopes of the pioneers were realized by the coming of the railroad in 1869. . . .

Father took a contract for the grading and masonry of 190 miles of road from the head of Echo Canyon to the lake shore. In order to complete the work by the time agreed upon, he needed some thousands of men more than could be spared from the farms, and so he wrote Franklin D. Richards, in charge of emigration abroad, to make arrangements with the steam ship lines so that the emigrants would arrive well ahead of schedule. . . .

His contract amounted to about two and one quarter million dollars, and some of this was sub-contracted to others, principally John Sharp and my brother Jospeh A. [Young], who did the heavy stone work of the bridge abutments, cut tunnels in Weber Canyon, and sent men into the mountains to cut timber for ties. . . .

It was on May 11, 1869, when the signal came that the last spike had been driven and the two iron horses stood nose to nose.[27]

"The Utah Iron Horse" and the three songs which follow— "Echo Canyon," "The Railroad Cars, They're Coming," and "The Iron Horse"—all date from the period of construction of the final link in the transcontinental railroad. The reader will note that a skeptical tone is present in the conclusion of this song—the railroad will bring evil as well as good.

The first published text of this song appeared in John Davis, *The Bee Hive Songster* (1868), pp. 26–27.

Mr. Avery, the man from whom I obtained the song, says that he had never seen it in print, that he learned the words from a railroad workman in Huntington, Utah, about 1900.

Text from William H. Avery, Blackfoot, Idaho, February, 1932.
Sung by Bob Christmas, Provo, Utah, January, 1960.
Other sources: 42 Fife 329–330; 43 Hubbard 453; 67 Emrich; 68 Fife MC I, 591 (Joseph H. Watkins, Brigham City, 1946).

> The Iron Horse draweth nigh
> With his smoke nostrils high,
> Eating fire while he blazes,
> Drinking water while he grazes.
> Then the steam rushes out,
> Whistles loud, "Clear the route,"
> For the Iron Horse is coming
> With the steam in his snout.
>
> Build him roads to come on,
> Make them level for the run,
> Dig tunnels through the mountains,
> Turn the currents of the fountains,
> Bridges build, stations make,
> Lay the track he will take,

---

[27] Spencer and Harmon, *One Who Was Valiant*, pp. 230–231.

37. *The Utah Iron Horse*

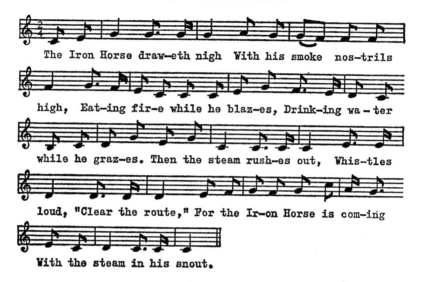

The Iron Horse draw—eth nigh With his smoke nos—trils high, Eat—ing fir—e while he blaz—es, Drink—ing wa—ter while he graz—es. Then the steam rush—es out, Whis—tles loud, "Clear the route," For the Ir—on Horse is com—ing With the steam in his snout.

For the iron horse is coming
With a train in his wake.

Civilized we will be,
Many people we shall see,
Lords and nobles, tramps and beggars,
Anyhow we'll see the niggers;
Saints will come, sinners too;
We'll have all we can do,
For the great Union Railroad
Will bring the Devil through.

38. *Echo Canyon*

The canyon east of Salt Lake City which gives this song its title is named, as one would expect, from the echo which attracted attention as sounds bounced off the mountains and returned. The ryhthm of the lyric is marked, simulating the rhythm of workmen striking the large railroad spikes with heavy hammers. Rosalie Sorrels and other singers have helped to make this song a present-day favorite.

38. *Echo Canyon*

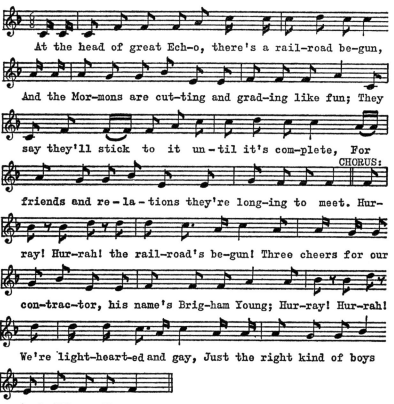

At the head of great Ech-o, there's a rail-road be-gun,

And the Mor-mons are cut-ting and grad-ing like fun; They

say they'll stick to it un-til it's com-plete, For

CHORUS:

friends and re-la-tions they're long-ing to meet. Hur-

ray! Hur-rah! the rail-road's be-gun! Three cheers for our

con-trac-tor, his name's Brig-ham Young; Hur-ray! Hur-rah!

We're light-heart-ed and gay, Just the right kind of boys

to build a rail-way.

Sung by L. M. Hilton, Ogden, Utah, July 18, 1959.
Other sources: 39 Durham 196; 43 Hubbard 451; 46 Ives 258–259; 67 Emrich; 68 Fife MC I, 571 (L. M. Hilton, Ogden, Utah, 1946); 70 Hilton; 71 Sorrels and Fife.

At the head of great Echo, there's a railroad begun,
And the Mormons are cutting and grading like fun;
They say they'll stick to it until it's complete,
For friends and relations they're longing to meet.

Chorus:
Hurray! Hurrah! The railroad's begun!
Three cheers for our contractor, his name's Brigham Young;

Hurray! Hurrah! We're lighthearted and gay,
Just the right kind of boys to build a railway.

Now there's Mr. Reed, he's a gentleman, too,
He knows very well what the Mormons can do;
He knows in our work we are faithful and true,
And if Mormon boys start it, it's bound to go through.

Our camp is united, we all labor hard,
And if we are faithful, we'll gain our reward;
Our leader is wise and a great leader, too,
And all things he tells us we are right glad to do.

The boys in our camp are lighthearted and gay,
We work on the railway ten hours a day;
We are thinking of fine times we'll have in the fall,
Then we'll be with our ladies and go to the ball.

We surely must live in a very fast age;
We've traveled by ox teams and then took the stage,
But when such conveyance is all done away,
We'll travel in steam cars upon the railway.

The great locomotive next season will come
To gather the Saints from their far distant home,
And bring them to Utah in peace here to stay
While the judgments of God sweep the wicked away.

ᏇᎧ 39. *The Railroad Cars, They're Coming* ᏇᎧ

Wording in this railroad song reflects more of a struggle for rhetoric than is shown in most folksong.

Text from Davidson, "Mormon Songs," Journal of American Folklore, *LVIII (October–December, 1945), 299, who obtained it from* Old Time Mormon and Far West Songs, *p. 35.*

> The great Pacific Railway,
>   For California hail!
> Bring on the locomotive,
>   Lay down the iron rail,

Across the rolling prairie,
'Mid mountain peaks so grand,
The railroad cars are steaming, gleaming
Through Mormon land,
The railroad cars are speeding, fleeting
Through Mormon land.

The prairie dogs in Dogtown,
Will wag their little tails,
When they see cars a-coming,
Just flying down the rails,
Amid the sav'ry sagebrush,
The antelope will stand,
While railroad cars go dashing, flashing,
Through Mormon land.

40. *The Iron Horse*

Whether this song is another version of "The Utah Iron Horse," Song No. 37, is not certain. The melody is not available. It is presented to show again the extent of the jubilation felt by the Utah people at completion of the transcontinental railroad.[28]

Text from Davidson, "Mormon Songs," Journal of American Folklore, *LVIII (October–December, 1945), 299, who obtained it from* Old Time Mormon and Far West Songs, *p. 52.*

The Iron Horse is coming here,
From out the East he's drawing near,
And we will at attention stand,
To welcome him to Mormon-land.

Across the plains the iron steed,
Into our valleys soon will speed,
He travels where he has a mind,
And draws a string of cars behind.

The Union railroad now is here,
And to the River brings us near,

[28] Another railroad song called "The Mormon Car" appears in the *Utah Humanities Review* of July, 1947, p. 298.

No more for months and months we'll wait,
For mules and ox-teams' slow-poke gait.

The Iron Horse snorts sparks and fire
And drinks ten barrels (and I'm no liar),
At twenty miles an hour he flies,
He runs a race on rails and ties.

41. *Bless Brigham Young*

Only a sampling of the mass of folksongs on Brigham Young
appears in this volume. Typical of a good many pro-Mormon songs
is the following from the Fife collection.

From Fife, Saints of Sage and Saddle, *p. 26 (Carolina Jensen,
Logan, Utah, 1946).*

*Other source: 68 Fife MC I, 566 (Mrs. Caroline Jensen, age 86,
Logan, Utah, 1946).*

> "Bless Brigham Young," we children pray,
> —"The chosen Twelve in what they say,
> The elders, priests, and teachers too,
> —Their labors bless in all they do.
>
> Let Thy good spirit on us rest,
> That one and all might thus be blessed,
> Unto our hearts with one accord,
> To comprehend thy will, oh Lord."

41. *Bless Brigham Young*

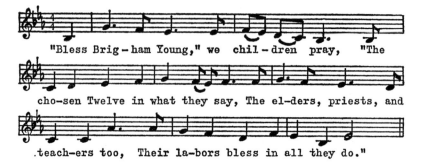

"Bless Brig–ham Young," we chil–dren pray, "The
cho–sen Twelve in what they say, The el–ders, priests, and
.teach–ers too, Their la–bors bless in all they do."

42. *Brigham Young's Birthday*

This eulogy of Brigham Young was composed by Charles L. Walker and sung first on June 1, 1876, to commemorate President Young's seventy-fifth birthday.

Copied from Charles L. Walker's journal, in possession of Kathryn M. Larson, St. George, Utah, July, 1960.

> God bless the chosen Seer
> To the Saints of God most dear,
> We rejoice to see his 75th birthday
> May blessings rich from Heaven
> Freely unto him be given
> And angels give him comfort night and day.
>
> *Chorus:*
> Oh God, bless thy servant, Brigham,
> Prolong his life for many a year
> To guide us to thy praise, we Saints of latter-days,
> And honest hearts in all the world to cheer.
>
> God's blessings on him send,
> On this world's best friend,
> Who so manfully has stood the trying hour.
> He's been faithful to his God
> And held fast the iron rod
> And almighty God has led him by his power.
>
> And may he live to see the power and majesty
> Of the Holy Priesthood reigning o'er the earth,
> And many Temples stand on this consecrated land
> And bless the goodly day that gave him birth.

43. *The Dying Prophet*

Having heard this song in my youth, I knew of its existence long before I collected the text. Sharon Garvey says that her grandfather, Joseph D. Packard, tells of hearing it sung many times. It concerns the last sickness, death, and funeral of Brigham Young. His loyalty and devotion to Joseph Smith during Joseph's life and after his death amounted to worshipful adoration. His last words as published immediately after his death were, "Joseph, Joseph, Joseph, Joseph."

Text from Sharon Garvey, Longview, Washington, October, 1964.

"Joseph, Joseph, Joseph, Joseph"; softly murmured Zion's
    chief,
As life's pulses weakened, ebbing, in the midst of loving
    grief;
Ah! the tale that tells is grander than the epics men
    have moved,
For it speaks of recognition; Joseph—was the man he loved!

He, the dying, prostrate leader, grasped in death the
    friend of yore,
Come to give a welcome greeting, as he neared the other
    shore;
Faithful, steadfast, tried and trusted, well thy mission thou
    hast done,
Joseph meets thee, on the threshold of the kingdom thou hast
    won!

True beside the great Ohio, true upon Missouri's plain,
True where Far West's prairies reaching, untouched by
    defection's stain;
True where Mississippi's waters glassed the Temple's towering
    dome,
True when Carthage sent its victims to their desolated home!

True when fleeing from the hunters, as the antelope flees by;
True when camped 'mid death and sorrow, 'neath the silent
    winter sky;
True in all that wondrous passage,—pilgrimage to peace,
    from strife,
True in Utah's proud dominions, marked by thy devoted life!

This the mission Jesus gave thee, Joseph on thy shoulders laid,
When his great heart quivered—feeling that his life would
    be betrayed;
So he passed in trust unshaken, as by revelation filled;
Joseph, Brigham, neither faltered, until death their efforts
    stilled.

And when murmuring softly—"Joseph," proudly thou could'st
    sink to rest,
On the outer verge of glory frankly greet "The Prophet" blest!
Ah, that meeting! who can grasp it, realize the surging swell,
Of those hearts who proved through all things that affection-
    acts best tell?

Who would falter? Mark their leader, emulate his life, his
    death;
Welcome they shall have when passing, greeting friends with
    latest breath;
Jesus, Joseph; Joseph, Brigham, 'twas triumphant music there;
Angel bands for introduction, every faithful soul shall share!

44. *The Mormon Tabernacle*

Through the years the turtle-topped tabernacle on Temple Square
in Salt Lake City has been a source of pride and joy to the people,
and its famed tabernacle organ is still a tourist attraction. The story
told in this song is a presentation in rhyme of facts which are told to
thousands of tourists every year.

When the tabernacle was built, soon after the Saints arrived in the
Valley, nails, bolts, and screws were unavailable. For that reason
timbers were put together with wooden pegs and rawhide bindings.
These have held solidly to this day. This detail is a striking fact
which the folk poet has presented interestingly in this song.

Sung by L. M. Hilton, Ogden, Utah, July 18, 1959.

> The Saints a tabernacle reared
> Where naught but sagebrush had appeared,
> Without a nail or bolt or screw
> Or anything to nail it to.
>
> A building destined to attract
> Attention from a world that lacked
> A single structure of the kind—
> No other like it can you find.
>
> They fabricated where they could
> Gigantic arches built of wood

44. *The Mormon Tabernacle*

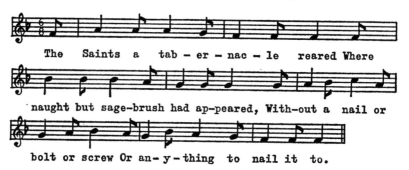

The Saints a tab - er - nac - le reared Where naught but sage-brush had ap-peared, With-out a nail or bolt or screw Or an- y - thing to nail it to.

Which afterwards they raised on high,
A wondrous sight there in the sky.

Then over all they laid a roof,
A curving lid made waterproof
Without supports of any kind
Except the arches I've defined.

The architect with modest pride
Then planned upon the great inside
A seating scheme unique and new
From which the speakers all could view.

An organ builder of the Saints,
Empowered to build without restraints,
Created as his dreams unfurled
A marvel of the organ world.

This house of such intrinsic worth
Is famous throughout all the earth
For its renowned acoustic roof;
That there's none like it stands the proof.

A whispered word from end to end
Of this huge structure will extend
And e'en a pin dropped where you like
Seems magnified into a spike.

Of all the marvels I recall
Connected with this Mormon hall

Is this strange fact that still prevails—
'Twas built without the use of nails.

With neither bolt, nor rod, nor screw,
For in those days such things were few.
A substitute was found as good—
'Twas built throughout with pegs of wood.

45. *The Gospel News Is Sounding*

Often one hears in Mormon circles statements such as, "Mormons hear more preaching than any people in the world." Harold Glen Clark published a book entitled *Millions of Meetings* telling of the profuse activity of the Church. This song is a preachment, a type of didacticism often heard in Mormon gatherings.

The music of this song as sung by Mr. Hilton, the contributor, is the same as that of Song No. 1. Mr. Hilton says the song "O'er the Lea," whose tune this song follows, is nine-hundred-years old, a bit of information that came from his parents from whom he got both this song and No. 1. Actually the melody hardly has the marks of such striking antiquity.

Sung by L. M. Hilton, Ogden, Utah, July 18, 1959.

Other sources: 68 Fife MC I, 582 (L. M. Hilton, Ogden, Utah, 1946); 71 Sorrels and Fife.

The Gospel news is sounding to nations far and near;
Good people pay attention and to its truth give ear,
For the Lord hath commissioned an angel from on high
A message bearing through the land and with it he did fly,
And with it he did fly, and with it he did fly,
A message bearing through the land, and with it he did fly.

Say now, give glory unto God who made the sea and land,
Repent of all your wickedness, God's judgments are at hand,
And then go forth with contrite hearts, believe in Jesus too,
And be baptized in His name and you shall know it's true,
And you shall know it's true, and you shall know it's true,
And be baptized in His name and you shall know it's true.

And then have hands laid on your head by those who God shall
     send,
You receive the Spirit's power 'twill guide you to the end,
'Twill show to you the things that's passed and things that's
     present too,
'Twill lead you through the wilderness, and nothing shall harm
     you,
And nothing shall harm you, and nothing shall harm you,
'Twill lead you through the wildnerness, and nothing shall
     harm you.

Receive the Priesthood of the Lord to act in Jesus' stead
And seal on earth and bind in Heaven the living and the dead,
And you shall heal the sick and cast out devils too,
And in new tongues you then shall speak and many things
     shall do,
And many things shall do, and many things shall do,
And in new tongues you then shall speak, and many things
     shall do.

Go forth and teach the Gospel plan to all by God's own power,
For Israel must be gathered in before the closing hour.
The wicked all must be destroyed and Satan must be bound,
And in that New Jerusalem the righteous will be found,
The righteous will be found, the righteous will be found,
And in that New Jerusalem the righteous will be found.

There'll be good old father Adam there and mother Eve his
     Queen,
And that innumerable company by John on Patmos will be
     seen.
There'll be Mary there and Martha too, with joy our hearts will
     swell;
Oh what a salutation we will have on Zion's hill,
Will have on Zion's hill, will have on Zion's hill;
Oh what a salutation we will have on Zion's hill.

In Zion's city there we'll build a temple to our Lord,
And Enoch's law will be our joy; we'll live in one accord.
The ten lost tribes will gather there with prophets long since
     dead;

A thousand years of peace will reign with Jesus at our head,
With Jesus at our head, with Jesus at our head;
A thousand years of peace will reign with Jesus at our head.

46. *Pioneer Day 1870*

Utah did not achieve statehood for many years after its population reached the required number. The reasons for this delay are two: first, the practice of polygamy; second, the political solidarity of the people—the Mormon political party, called the People's Party, could win any election in the state. When Utah finally became a state on January 4, 1896, the Church itself had taken measures to split the people into Democratic and Republican camps.

This song reflects Mormon thinking regarding the unkindness of "Uncle Sam" in denying them a state. The unhappiness of the Utah citizens did not bring about the acquiring of statehood until more than twenty-five years after this song was first sung.

Composed by Charles L. Walker and copied from his journal, in possession of Kathryn M. Larson, St. George, Utah, May, 1960. Sung by Bob Christmas, Berkeley, California, May 17, 1962.

>Dear friends, I pray just lend an ear
>Whilst I relate a song,
>I do not mean disloyalty
>Or anything that's wrong.
>But all of you will bear me out
>In what I now relate,
>That Uncle Sam has been unkind
>In denying us a state.
>
>*Chorus:*
>Then shout and sing for Zion's sons,
>Three cheers for Deseret,
>Although they've tried to kill us all,
>We're all alive as yet.
>
>Just three and twenty years have passed
>If I do not mistake,
>Since a noble band of pioneers

46. *Pioneer Day 1870*

First gazed upon Salt Lake.
They built the bridges, made the roads
And left their homes behind;
Their tracks were marked by stains of blood
In fleeing from mankind.

We'd just commenced to build a town
When Bracchus raised a row
And Brandenburg helped him out
As well as he knew how.
But Brigham crooked this little thing [little finger]
And that soon stopped the fuss,
Then Brandenburg sneaked off home,
Also the other cuss.

To heap insult upon the Saints
Judge Drummond on the bench
Placed a lewd woman by his side,
A common strumpet wench,
And Steptoe thought to crush us down
And over us hold sway,
But he got foiled and badly whipped
All on a Christmas day.

In fifty-seven the army came
To kill us all, you know;
God placed a hook right in their jaws
And kept them in the snow.
Whilst we, a few rough Mormon boys,
Thought we'd give them relief
By burning trains and driving stock
And killing us some beef.

How much they suffered in the snow
No mortal tongue can tell;
They wandered up and down Ham's Fork
And wished the Saints in Hell.
While we were all quite blithe and gay
Not fearing Johnston's fools,
The flower of Uncle Sam's Army
Was feasting on dead mules.

In fifty-eight they marched in town
And looked down in the mouth;
The streets and houses were empty;
The Saints had all moved South.
And thus we gained a victory
At their expense and fun
And whipped out Jim Buchanan's crowd
And never fired a gun.

Judge Titus Cradlebaugh and company
With Pat Connor at their head
And a host of army contractors
All wished the Mormons dead
And urged the Government to send more troops,
More rogues and pimps;

We wished them all a good warm place
With Satan and his imps.

And lastly Poland and his crowd
Thought it was wondrous wise
To introduce in Washington
A bill to disenfranchise
The Mormon people of their rights
And send them all to jail
For marrying in Celestial law,
Oh, how we fear and quail!

They say the bill has passed the House
And also the Senate late.
Should Congress make the bill a law
We'll make ourselves a state;
With Brigham Young true at the helm
We'll ride o'er rocks and shoals,
And Congress cannot help themselves
To save their precious souls.

God bless the noble pioneers,
God bless the 24th
And all our thriving settlements
From extreme South to North.
God bless the old battalion boys
Who went to Mexico,
God bless the Saints in Dixieland,
And God bless Brother Snow.

47. All Are Talking of Utah

Whether the folk poet John Davis, who wrote under the pseudonym of Ieuan, presented in this song a factual account of Utah's notoriety in the nation is questionable. But it appears evident that he caught the spirit of the Mormon folk. This song, like the preceding one, is about the problems of polygamy and Utah's becoming a state. The pride of Mormons for Mormonism, their group loyalty, and their derision of governmental disapproval of the practice of polygamy are characteristics of the people demonstrated in basic folk ways.

From William Willes, The Mountain Warbler *(1872), pp. 66–67.*
Other sources: 36 Davis 37; 44 Hubbard 127.
Tune: "Marching Through Georgia"

Who'd ever think that Utah would stir the world so much,
Who'd ever think the Mormons were widely known as such,
I hardly dare to scribble, or such a subject touch,
    For all are talking of Utah.

Chorus:
Hurrah, hurrah, the Mormons have a name,
Hurrah, hurrah, they're on the road to fame;
Don't matter what they style us
It's all about the same,
    For all are talking of Utah.

'Tis Utah and the Mormons, in Congress, pulpit, press,
'Tis Utah and the Mormons, in every place, I guess;
We must be growing greater, we can't be growing less,
    For all are talking of Utah.

They say they'll send an army to set the Mormons right,
Regenerate all Utah, and show us Christian light;
Release our wives and daughters, and put us men to fight,
    For all are talking of Utah.

They say that Utah cannot be numbered as a State,
They wished our lands divided, but left it rather late;
'Tis hard to tell of Mormons, what yet may be their fate,
    For all are talking of Utah.

Whatever may be coming, we cannot well forsee,
For it may be the Railroad, or some great prodigy;
At least the noted Mormons are watching what's to be,
    For all are talking of Utah.

I now will tell you something you never thought of yet,
We bees are nearly filling the "Hive of Deseret."
If hurt we'll sting together, and gather all we get,
    For all are talking of Utah.

୧୬ 48. *Conference Time* ୧୬

Traditionally the Mormons have held a semiannual (April and October) General Conference in Salt Lake City for all Church members. The song presented here gives a local-color picture of folk customs at conference time in 1895. Free lodging in the tithing barn and a fifteen-cent breakfast are economies worth singing about.

Sung by Don Wakefield, Huntington, Utah, June 8, 1958.
Tune: "Vilikins and His Dinah."

How many old-timers remember the day
When attending the conference with no place to stay,
We slept in the hay in the tithing-yard barn
And awakening time was like resurrection morn.

How many were there, I often have wondered.
For all who slept there never was numbered.
But those who were rich and considered quite swell,
They rented a room in the Cullen Hotel.

The rest of us, though, with no place to flop
Were never once bothered by any old cop.
At day break we'd out and shinny a fence,
And buy a swell breakfast for fifteen cents.

And then after breakfast, with money to spare,
We'd high tail it back to the Old Temple Square.
With folks there from Manti and others from Morgan
We'd sit there enthralled by the wonderful organ.

When it came time for lunch and our spirits ran high
We'd buy cheese and crackers at Z.C.M.I.
I wonder how many are still alive—
It was the year eighteen ninety-five.

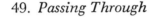 49. *Passing Through*

The original of this recent composition of the folksinging revival lends itself readily to new verses. The last three stanzas in this version are Mormon additions. These stanzas deal in turn with each of three presidents of the Church (designated also as prophets). Each stanza deftly states a prominent legendary fact for which the man is known and also fittingly characterizes him in dialogue.

Some people in the Church believed so keenly that polygamous living was what God wanted of them that they found it difficult to accept the Manifesto, the proclamation which prohibited the practice. The defense Wilford Woodruff made for issuing the order as given in the song is accepted as historical truth in the Church.

Sung by Bob Christmas, Provo, Utah, January 11, 1960.

49. *Passing Through*

I saw Ad-am leave that gar-den with an ap-ple in his hand, I said, "Now you're out, well, what you goin' to do?" "Well, I'll plant my crops and pray for rain, may-be raise a lit-tle cane; I'm an or-phan now and on-ly pass-ing through." Pass-ing through, pass-ing through, Some-times hap-py, some-times blue, Glad that I ran in-to you, Tell the peo-ple that you saw me pass-ing through."

I saw Adam leave that garden with an apple in his hand,
I said, "Now you're out, well, what you goin' to do?"
"Well, I'll plant my crops and pray for rain, maybe raise
    a little cane;
I'm an orphan now and only passing through."

Chorus:
"Passing through, passing through,
Sometimes happy, sometimes blue,
Glad that I ran into you,
Tell the people that you saw me passing through."

I saw Jesus on that cross, on that hill called Calvary,
"Do you hate mankind for what they've done to you?"
He said, "Talk of love, not hate, things to do, it's getting
    late,
There's so little time and we're all passing through."

I was at Franklin Roosevelt's side just the night before he
    died,
And he said, "One world must come from World War II,
Yankee, Russian, white or tan, Lord, a man is just a man,
We're all brothers and we're only passing through."

I saw Joseph dig those plates from that hill in New York State;
"Do you realize what men will say of you?"
He said, "Though I'm called a fraud, still this book must go
    abroad,
'Cause it testifies that we're all passing through."

I stood by the prophet's carriage when he said, "This is the
    place—"
I asked, "Brigham, are you sure that you speak true?"
He said, "Though this valley's dry, it'll flower by and by;
Here the Saints will live while they're all passing through.

When the Manifesto came, I watched Wilford sign his name,
I said, "Future Saints will all depend on you—"
He said, "God has shown me why the Church must follow this
    or die—
We'll obey the law while we're all passing through."

Songs of Mormon Country Locale

If life was hard in Teton Basin, Idaho, where I was born and where my parents pioneered, it was doubly hard in some other more arid regions of the intermountain West. My parents sang "Waste Not, Want Not" with feeling, yet they always had water for irrigation and my mother has no memories of being without bread. Mormon settlers in the St. George, Utah, area could sing songs of frugality with deep feeling, for they experienced abject poverty. "'Tis seven weeks last Sunday since I have tasted bread," wrote George Hicks. One reason why colonizers of St. George have left such a striking legacy of folksong is that there were several superior creative singers and writers among those who were "called" to go there. The songs they wrote were not all on conquering the desert; they also wrote about temple-building and other religious and secular events and problems.

Areas of Mormon country represented here which are far from St. George are Logan, Cache County, in northern Utah; Sanpete, Juab, and Utah Counties, all in central Utah; Heber, Wasatch County, just east of Salt Lake County; Monticello, in southeastern Utah; and Teton County, in southeast Idaho.

The songs from these areas show much in common with those from St. George; yet other items are added, including local events, freighting, and a strong emphasis on love for the beauty of external nature.

⟨flourish⟩ 50. *St. George and the Drag-on* ⟨flourish⟩

The Church leaders planned to build a self-sustaining empire in the Great Basin. To secure the Basin and its approaches, settlements were established on all outposts. Utah's southland, the Rio Virgin Valley, was called Utah's Dixie. It was not only an outpost but a place where cotton and silk could be produced to supply the needs of the Church. Accordingly, families were called officially by the Church leaders to go to the Rio Virgin area. Since it was very dry (a mean average rainfall of only 6.31 inches measured between 1893 and 1901), the settlers faced extreme hardship.

The name of this song, a pun on an English folksong, "Saint George and the Dragon," shows vividly the "drag-on" year after year of the fight for sustenance. The song was written about 1870 by an early pioneer, Charles L. Walker, and first sung in a concert at which George A. Smith, the man for whom the town of St. George was named, and Brigham Young were visitors. The song catches the spirit of pioneering so well that it has been found in oral circulation in many areas of the West.

In literary quality it has few superiors in folksong; its epic exaggeration, its rhyme and rhythm, its tone of hopeful gaiety mixed with the pathos of hardship, its folk idiom, its direct and terse presentation, its musical lyric which amplifies the words—all of these make this one of the best folksongs of Mormondom.

Composed by Charles L. Walker and copied from his journal, in possession of Kathryn M. Larson, St. George, Utah, May, 1960.

Sung by Bob Christmas, Provo, Utah, January 1, 1960.

Other sources: 42 Fife 330; 63 Swan 41–42; 64 Swan 244–245; 67 Emrich; 68 Fife MC I, 641 (R. McArthur, St. George, Utah, 1946); 71 Sorrels and Fife.

Oh, what a desert place was this
When first the Mormons found it;
They said no white man here could live
And Indians prowl'd around it.
They said the land it was no good,
And the water was no gooder,
And the bare idea of living here
Was enough to make one shudder.

Chorus:
Mesquite, soap root, prickly-pears and briars,
St. George ere long will be a place that everyone admires.

Now green lucerne in verdant spots
Bedecks our thriving city,
Whilst vines and fruit trees grace our lots

50. *St. George and the Drag-On*

Oh, what a des-ert place was this When first the Mor-mons found it; They said no white man here could live And In - dians prowl'd a - round it. They said the land it was no good, And the wa - ter was no good - er, And the bare i-dea of liv-ing here Was e-nough to make one shud-der.

CHORUS: Mes - quite, soap root, prick-ly-pears and bri-ars, St. George ere long will be a place that ev-ery one ad-mires.

With flowers sweet and pretty.
Where once the grass in single blades
Grew a mile apart in distance,
And it kept the crickets on the go
To pick up their subsistence.

The sun it is so scorching hot
It makes the water siz, Sir,
The reason why it is so hot
Is just because it is, Sir.
The wind like fury here does blow
That when we plant or sow, Sir,
We place one foot upon the seed
And hold it till it grows, Sir.

51. Marching to Dixie

Many of the songs in this collection refer to being "called." This means that the president of the Church has officially asked the person to respond. Since the president is the prophet, the call is interpreted by loyal followers as "the will of the Lord." To refuse to accept the call is, therefore, evidence of lack of faith. One can see in this song the folk attitude toward those who fail to follow counsel: "They're on the road to Hell."

Mormons are said to be the "prayingest" people in the world. In the Church all meetings as well as all entertainments are opened and closed with prayer. This song, although put to the rhythmic vigor of "Marching Through Georgia," ends with a prayer for Dixie Mormons and the Church leaders.

Composed by Charles L. Walker and copied from his journal, in possession of Kathryn M. Larson, St. George, Utah, August, 1960. Tune: "Marching Through Georgia."

> Some six or seven years ago this country looked forlorn,
> A God-forsaken country as sure as you are born.
> The lizards crept around it and thorns universal had grown
> As we came marching to Dixie.
>
> *Chorus:*
> Hurrah! Hurrah! The thorns we have cut down.
> Hurrah! Hurrah! We're building quite a town.
> St. George is growing greater and gaining great renown,
> Since we came marching to Dixie.
>
> The land was white with mineral, the water tasted mean,
> 'Twas the most forbidding country that men had ever seen.
> Our stint was to subdue it and make things neat and green
> As we came marching to Dixie.
>
> A number that were called here, their names I shall not tell,
> Thought more of their notions and were afraid to sell,
> But if I am not mistaken, they're on the road to Hell
> Since we came marching to Dixie.
>
> There's a certain man in Utah whose faith began to fail,
> He's measured Mormon Dixie by the breadth of his thumb nail;

Now when he gets converted, he'll tell a truer tale
When he comes marching to Dixie.

We built the Virgin Ditch, which has often us perplexed,
It furnishes us with sermons and very often texts,
It has often made us weary and very often vexed
As we were toiling in Dixie.

We have battled with the mineral, we've battled with our foes,
We've battled with the Virgin, that everybody knows,
Our desert homes are pretty and blossom like the rose
Since we came marching to Dixie.

God bless the Dixie Mormons, wherever they may go,
God bless our prophet, Brigham, the Twelve, and Rastus Snow,
Likewise our wives and children, and all the saints we know
As they came marching to Dixie.

⊙⥹⊙ 52. *St. George and Mormon Dixie* ⊙⥹⊙

*Composed by Charles L. Walker and copied from his journal, in
possession of Kathryn M. Larson, St. George, Utah, August, 1960.
Sung by Kathryn and Karl Larson, April 17, 1960.
Tune: "Annie Laurie."*

St. George is bright and sunny,
Its cloudless skies are blue,
Its flowers are fair and bonnie,
Its faithful Saints are true,
It blossoms like the rose
Where once the cactus grew,
For St. George and Mormon Dixie
I hope we'll all prove true.

Its rocks are black and red, Sir,
Its scenery is grand,
The mineral kills things dead, Sir,

That ain't piled up with sand.
The wind blows hard and long,
The sand in clouds does fly,
For St. George and Mormon Dixie
I'd rather live than die.

53. *Once I Lived in Cottonwood*

Few songs of Mormondom speak more potent truth than this one.
It is a favorite because of its universal appeal. Every man can see
something of himself in the reactions of George Hicks to an antag-
onistic environment.

Cottonwood was a fertile farming area just south of Salt Lake City.
The composer of this song had settled there and had established a
prosperous farm when he was called to "Dixie." It was a hard call
to accept and a harder one to fulfill, for he and his family were in-
creasingly bludgeoned with the hostile forces of nature.

This song was published in a humor magazine in Salt Lake City
called *The Keepapitchinin,* May 1, 1870.

Written by George Hicks.
Sung by Andrew Karl Larson, St. George, Utah, April 17, 1960.
Other sources: 39 Durham 94; 44 Hubbard 430; 54 Lomax 182–
184; 64 Swan 40–41; 68 Fife MC I, 671 (Francis Y. Morse, St.
George, Utah, 1947); three other listings in the Fife Collection; 71
Sorrels and Fife.

Oh, once I lived in Cottonwood and owned a little farm,
But I was called to Dixie, which did me much alarm;
To raise the cane and cotton, I right away must go;
But the reason why they called on me, I'm sure I do not know.

I yoked old Jim and Bolly up all for to make a start,
To leave my house and garden, it almost broke my heart.
We moved along quite slowly and often looked behind,
For the sand and rocks of Dixie kept running through my mind.

At length we reached the Black Ridge where I broke my
    wagon down,
I could not find a carpenter so far from any town,

53. *Once I Lived in Cottonwood*

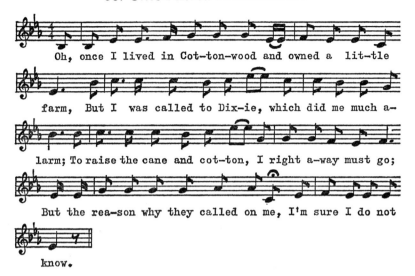

Oh, once I lived in Cot-ton-wood and owned a lit-tle farm, But I was called to Dix-ie, which did me much a-larm; To raise the cane and cot-ton, I right a-way must go; But the rea-son why they called on me, I'm sure I do not know.

So with a clumsy cedar pole I fixed an awkward slide;
My wagon pulled so heavy then that Betsy could not ride.

While Betsy was a'walking, I told her to take care,
When all upon a sudden she struck a prickly pear.
Then she began to blubber out as loud as she could bawl,
"If I was back in Cottonwood, I would not come at all!"

When we reached the Sandy, we could not move at all,
For poor old Jim and Bolly began to puff and loll.
I whipped and swore a little but could not make the route,
For myself, the team, and Betsy, were all of us give out.

Next we got to Washington, where we stayed a little while
To see if April showers would make the verdure smile.
But, oh, I was mistaken and so I went away,
For the red hills of November looked just the same in May.

I feel so weak and hungry now, there's nothing here to cheer
Except prophetic sermons which we very often hear.
They will hand them out by dozens and prove them by the book—
I'd rather have some roasting ears to stay at home and cook.

I feel so weak and hungry now, I think I'm nearly dead;
'Tis seven weeks next Sunday since I have tasted bread.

Of carrot tops and lucerne greens we have enough to eat—
But I'd like to change that diet off for buckwheat cakes and meat.

I brought this old coat with me about two years ago,
And how I'll get another one, I'm sure I do not know.
May providence protect me against the cold and wet;
I think myself and Betsy, these times will not forget.

My shirt is dyed with wild dockroot, with greasewood for a set;
I fear the colors all will fade when once it does get wet.
They said we could raise madder, and indigo so blue,
But that turned out a humbug, the story was not true.

The hot winds whirl around me and take away my breath;
I've had the chills and fever till I'm nearly shook to death.
"All earthly tribulations are but a moment here;
And, oh, if I prove faithful, a righteous crown I'll wear."

My wagon's sold for sorghum seed to make a little bread;
And poor old Jim and Bolly long ago are dead.
There's only me and Betsy left to hoe the cotton-tree;
May Heaven help the Dixie-ite wherever he may be!

54. *The Drunkards of Bonanza*

The contributor of this song gives the following matrix:

My grandfather, Hyrum Leany, was a small man born in 1852 in
Parowan, Iron County, Utah. His parents were called to the Dixie Cot-
ton Mission by the Latter Day Saints Church in the 1860's. After the
Civil War, these Saints were advised to raise produce. Specifically they
raised grapes which they preserved as wine for shipment. This proved
a fearsome temptation for the Saints, many of whom in tasting their
brew decided not to ship the best away.

About 1879 silver was discovered in a sandstone formation in the area.
Miners from Nevada and California hurried to the mine which was
named Silver Reef. Close by this mining town another one named
Bonanza was also established. These "wild and woolley" mining towns
in close proximity with the staid Mormon settlements led to an interesting interchange of action. The Mormons became more worldly and the
mining camps surprisingly more settled. In a year or so all of the silver
claims were held by large eastern mining companies and the miners

were often the local Mormon people. My grandfather was one of these miners.

"Hy" Leany was thirty-six years old when he married a tall slender girl of eighteen. This girl, Mary Elizabeth Woodbury, was very religious and serious and did much to calm down grandfather's boisterous, mining-camp spirit. They had eleven children, nine of them boys. For thirty-seven years grandfather served in the local ward bishopric as a counselor. In his later years he became a regular temple worker in the Saint George Temple that he helped build as a young man. He was a very active and busy man until his death at ninety-four.

Yet despite these fifty years of marriage and his large family, he never quite overcame his old songs, stories, and tricks. He loved to play battery rook all night with his grandsons or take all the boys to swim in the irrigation canals. He was a frequent program entertainer. He always liked to dance a soft-shoe and sing one of the drinking songs he had helped to create. In fact, no program needed to be planned—he would be glad to start one on the moment.

"The Drunkards of Bonanza" was one of "Hy" Leany's favorites. There is not one of his children who doesn't remember his father singing it.

This song was probably composed under the influence of Dixie wine by Father Tom McNelly and others. Father McNelly came to Silver Reef as spiritual advisor for the Gillespie brothers. He arrived at the mining camp driving an unmatched team—one horse and one jackass. Father McNelly was a natural humorist and rhymster, like Hy Leany, who often sang the songs the religious leader wrote.

Mel Laney, who collected the song from his uncles, the sons of Hy Leany, says: "All of the nine sons of Hy Leany seem to have inherited his unusual sense of humor, but not a one could sing or dance a soft shoe. After listening to several of the brothers try to sing what they thought was the melody their father used, I composed a melody."

Text from Mel Laney, November, 1964.

> In ancient days they came to pass
> Two men who drove a horse and ass,
> They came to mine, but alas, alas,
> They spread about Bonanza.
>
> They called on Stirling oft and long,
> The captain treated, which was wrong
> Because there was an awful throng,
> Of bummers from Bonanza.

The way they acted was a shame,
And each of them did loudly claim,
That Lusk and Robb were known to fame [Bill Lusk
   and Wm. Robb]
As outcasts from Bonanza.

For men, you know they will deceive,
And drink, and smile way up their sleeve;
Get wine on tick from Joe McCleave,
Them topers from Bonanza.

Jack Kirby scraped at Stirling's song [played violin]
And the boys said something far from wrong
Which upset all that awful throng
Of bummers from Bonanza.

An old Piocher then came in, [from Pioche, Nevada]
And said, "Old Pard, this is too thin;
We'll drink no slush, but straight up gin,
You suckers from Bonanza.

Walt and Ben were on it, too [Walter Dodge and Ben
   Paddock]
And Cunningham, who'd had a few;
They'd fall for any kind of brew,
Them drunkards from Bonanza.

And anyone who looks will find,
Old Homan is not far behind;
His smelter smoke will graceful wind [smoke from
   his tobacco pipe]
And float toward Bonanza.

Then, in came the Gypsy Boss,
Who gave his carrot head a toss,
The boys then yelled, "Go in, old Hoss!
And bully for Bonanza."

ᏬᎥᏉ 55. *Lo a Temple* ᏬᎥᏉ

Temples of the Church are not just meetinghouses. They are used for sacred ordinances for the salvation of the living and the dead. Mormons say that biblical teachings indicate that only those who are baptized may be saved: "Except a man be born of the water and of the spirit, he cannot enter the kingdom of God." Mormons believe in salvation for all mankind. Those who die without a Mormon baptism may have opportunity to accept a proxy ordinance performed for them in a temple. Mormons give support for this belief and practice by reference to both biblical and modern revelation. They claim that proxy baptism was practiced in the Apostolic Church following the time of Christ and cite Scripture to support the belief, the most striking of which is Paul's statement, "Else what shall they do which are baptized for the dead if the dead rise not at all? Why then are they baptized for the dead?"

The ordinance of baptism for the dead is performed in the temples, as are other secret ordinances designed to assist the recipient (both the living and the dead) to eternal exaltation. The reader may note the reference to this doctrine in this song and in the following songs related to temples.

This song was sung not only in the St. George area, but also throughout Mormondom to encourage people to donate work or money toward completion of the St. George Temple.

Composed by Charles L. Walker and copied from his journal, in possession of Kathryn M. Larson, St. George, Utah, April 17, 1960. Sung by Kathryn M. Larson, St. George, Utah, April 17, 1960. Other sources: 63 Swan 43; 68 Fife MC I, 693 (Jane Moss, St. George, 1947).

Lo a Temple long expected in St. George shall stand
By God's faithful Saints erected here in Dixie land.

Chorus:
Hallelujah, hallelujah, let hosannas ring,
Heaven shall echo back our praises, Christ shall reign as King.

The noble task we hailed with pleasure, coming from our head
Brings salvation, life eternal for our kindred dead.

Holy and Eternal Father, give us strength we pray
To thy name to build his Temple in the latter day.

55. *Lo a Temple*

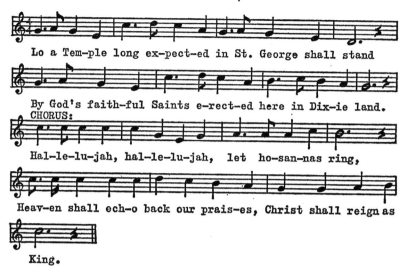

Lo a Tem-ple long ex-pect-ed in St. George shall stand

By God's faith-ful Saints e-rect-ed here in Dix-ie land.

CHORUS:

Hal-le-lu-jah, hal-le-lu-jah, let ho-san-nas ring,

Heav-en shall ech-o back our prais-es, Christ shall reign as

King.

Oh, how anxious friends are waiting, watching every move
Made by us for their redemption with a holy love.

Long they've hoped through weary ages of the prison time
For the everlasting gospel with its truth sublime.

Lo, the prison doors are open, millions hail the day
Praying, hoping for baptism in the appointed way.

Glory, glory hallelujah, let the structure rise,
Rear aloft these noble towers pointing to the skies.

Ꮿ 56. *Pounding Rock into the Temple Foundation* Ꮿ

Construction of the St. George Temple, the subject of this song, was begun in 1871. The song gives a vivid picture of the local method of building a solid foundation.

Composed by Charles L. Walker and copied from his journal, in possession of Kathryn M. Larson, St. George, Utah, April 18, 1960. Tune: "Cork Leg."

Now I pray you be still and I'll hush your noise
While I sing about Carter and the pounder and boys,
Now the old hammer climbed and went toward the skies
And made such a thump that you'd shut both your eyes.

Go ahead now, hold hard, now snatch it again.
Down comes the old gun, the rocks fly like rain.
Now start up the team, we've worked not in vain
With rattle and clatter and do it again.

Slack upon the south, the north guy make tight,
Take a turn round the post, now be sure you are right.
Now stick in your bars and drive your dogs tight,
Slap dope in the grooves, go ahead, all is right.

Now right on the grama sat the giant Jimmy Ide
Like a brave engineer with the rope by his side.
"Go ahead and just raise it," he lustily cried,
"I run this machine and Carter besides."

I must not forget to mention our Rob
Who stuck to it faithful and finished the job
The time it fell down and nearly played hob,
He ne'er made a whimper, not even a sob.

Here's goodwill to Carter, the pounder and tools,
Here's goodwill to Gardner, the driver and mules,
Here's goodwill to the boys for they've had a hard tug,
Here's goodwill to us all and the little brown jug.

57. Song for the Temple Volunteers

Again in this song Charles L. Walker, the local poet of St. George, catches the spirit of the folk. Building "temples in Zion" was, and still is, an obsession with Mormon people. The Saints continue to teach and to feel the elation that comes from doing what they believe will bring "eternal blessings from Heaven."

Composed by Charles L. Walker and copied from his journal, in possession of Kathryn M. Larson, St. George, Utah.
Sung by Kathryn M. Larson, St. George, Utah, April 17, 1960.
Tune: "Marching Through Georgia."

Ye Saints throughout the mountains, pray listen to my rhyme
Of a noble band of brethren who came to Dixie's clime
To build a holy Temple just in a stated time
As they were counseled by Brigham.

Chorus:
Hurrah! Hurrah! Hurrah for Brigham Young!
Hurrah for all the noble boys who pushed the work along!
God bless them in their labors and all their lives prolong
To build up temples in Zion.

They left their homes and firesides responsive to the call
And labored hard and faithful to rear the Temple's walls.
Their union and their oneness was seen and felt by all
Who labored to build up the Temple.

They little think the work they've done, the glory it will lead
And be the means of saving some thousands of our dead
And bring eternal blessings of Heaven upon their heads
And stand as saviours in Zion.

58. Logan Temple

Only active, tithe-paying, church-attending, nondrinking, non-smoking, loyal members are admitted in temples, and no nonmember may enter. The last stanza of this song is an accurate statement of what temple work is and what motivates it among faithful mem-

58. *Logan Temple*

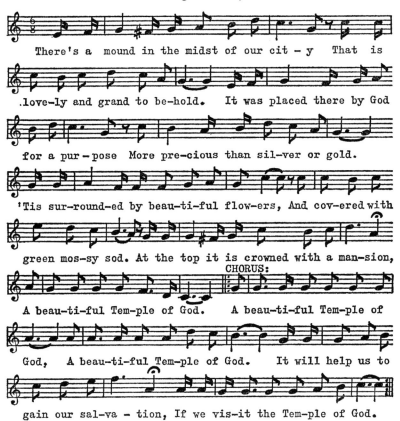

There's a mound in the midst of our cit-y That is .love-ly and grand to be-hold. It was placed there by God for a pur-pose More pre-cious than sil-ver or gold. 'Tis sur-round-ed by beau-ti-ful flow-ers, And cov-ered with green mos-sy sod. At the top it is crowned with a man-sion, A beau-ti-ful Tem-ple of God.

CHORUS:

A beau-ti-ful Tem-ple of God, A beau-ti-ful Tem-ple of God. It will help us to gain our sal-va - tion, If we vis-it the Tem-ple of God.

bers. To those who dedicate themselves to temple work, the temples are the embodiment of peace and beauty.

Text contributed by the composer, H. G. Stevens, Logan, Utah, 1959.

> There's a mound in the midst of our city
> That is lovely and grand to behold.
> It was placed there by God for a purpose
> More precious than silver or gold.
> 'Tis surrounded by beautiful flowers,
> An covered with green, mossy sod.

At the top it is crowned with a mansion,
A beautiful Temple of God.

Chorus:
A beautiful Temple of God,
A beautiful Temple of God.
It will help us to gain our salvation
If we visit the Temple of God.

It was built there of stone from the mountains
And has stood now for many long years,
By direct revelation from heaven,
It was built by the old pioneers.
It has served its great purpose for thousands,
Who have come there from near and afar,
And has helped them to gain their salvation
No matter whoever they are.

It was built there for giving endowments,
To the living as well as the dead,
And these are the things that's celestial
As the Prophet Elijah has said.
So let's visit that beautiful Temple
That we may be saviours above,
It will help us to gain our salvation
And again meet the ones that we love.

59. *We the Boys of Sanpete County*

In 1868 Brigham Young sent William Stewart Seeley of Mount Pleasant, Utah, with forty wagons manned by young men to the Laramie, Wyoming, area to assist a party of immigrants en route to Salt Lake Valley. The tragedy which came to the young men as they crossed Green River is recounted in this historically true song. The song has been sung by many people both in the Sanpete area and elsewhere in the Church.

Sung by M. E. Wakefield, Ogden, Utah, August 13, 1959.
Other sources: 44 Hubbard 404; 51 Laws, "The Boys of Sanpete County," B26; 68 Fife MC I, 597; (Mrs. Elva Christensen, Manti, Utah, 1946).

Tune: "Just Before the Battle, Mother."

We the boys of Sanpete County, in obedience to the call,
Started out with forty wagons to bring immigrants in the fall,
Without fear or thought of danger lightly on our way we sped,
Every heart with joy abounded, Captain Seeley at the head.

Chorus:
To accomplish our mission, we were called to fill below,
Left our friends and dear relations, on the dreary plains to go.

When we reached Green River Ferry, on its banks all night we
    stayed,
In the morning we ferried our wagons over, thinking soon to roll
    away;
Next to drive the cattle over, but we found they could not swim,
And O, the boys were in the water many hours up to their chin.

Some to oxen's horns were clinging but to them it was all o'er,
Boys and cattle all went under never more to step on shore;
Some to planks and boards were clinging down the swelling tide
    did float,
But some by heaven seemed protected driven to shore upon the
    boat.

One had landed on an island was clinging to the willows green,
But to him life seemed extinguished and he backward fell into the
    stream.
Thus six boys from parents parted and from friends that they did
    love,
Yet there is a brighter morning where we all shall meet above.

Chorus:
Farewell parents we will never meet you on this earth again.
But there is a brighter morning when we all shall meet again.

ᠳ᠑ 60. *Down in Utah* ᠳ᠑

Often quoted in Mormon church services is the biblical passage,
"For I am not ashamed of the Gospel of Christ, for it is the power
of God unto salvation to all those that believe." For a Mormon not
to confess he is a Mormon is considered tantamount to refusal to
accept Christ. During the period in which Mormons were maligned
and hated, saying "I'm a Mormon" was a challenge to an enemy of
the Church, even though it might be a triumph for the Mormon.

This song, which no doubt originated in Sanpete County, Utah,
was taken from a tape recording made by Job Porter of Victor, Idaho,
shortly before his death in 1958. It was contributed by his daughter,
Helen Dewolf of Jackson, Wyoming, in July 1959.

Sung by Job Porter, Victor, Idaho, July, 1957.

> While the workmen stopped in Denver
> One fellow came to me—
> Said he, "Are you from Utah,
> And why are you so free?"
> I smiled and said, "Young fellow,
> Unless you break my jaw,
> I'm a Mormon man with residence in Utah."
>
> *Chorus*:
> And if you are from Utah,
> They'll often question you
> All about the hated Mormons
> And really what they do.
> Some have a bad opinion
> While others pick a flaw;
> They think we live on carrots down in Utah.
>
> We had it hot and heavy
> 'Til both were getting sick,
> My eyes were getting black and blue
> And my lips were getting thick,
> But I stayed with my young smarty
> 'Til he was getting raw,
> And the battle fell in favor of old Utah.
>
> I know I was a-sweating
> And looking mighty blue

60. *Down in Utah*

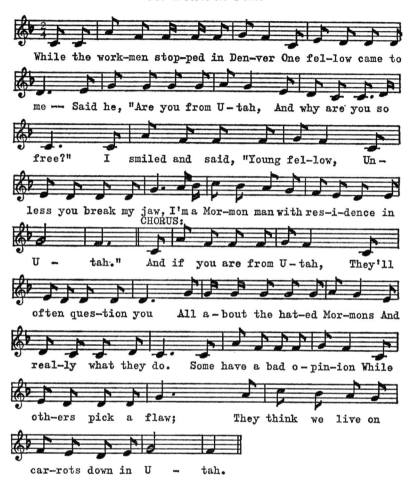

While the work-men stop-ped in Den-ver One fel-low came to
me — Said he, "Are you from U-tah, And why are you so
free?" I smiled and said, "Young fel-low, Unless you break my jaw, I'm a Mor-mon man with res-i-dence in

CHORUS:

U - tah." And if you are from U-tah, They'll
often ques-tion you All a-bout the hat-ed Mor-mons And
real-ly what they do. Some have a bad o-pin-ion While
oth-ers pick a flaw; They think we live on
car-rots down in U - tah.

When a cop comes stepping up to me,
Said he, "I'm on to you."
I smiled and looked upon him
While he held me in his claw,
And the battle fell in favor of old Utah.

We rode along together
Down to the city hall.
'Twas there I met my smarty

I scarcely knew at all.
The cop he said, "Young fellow,
To you I'll read the law."
And the battle fell in favor of old Utah.

61. *My House*

This fragment composed by the grandmother of Mrs. Foreman
has been sung by the family for three generations.

Sung by Naomi Foreman, Moreland, Idaho, July 28, 1958.

My house it is built by an old sheep corral,
And I've lived there so long I've got used to the smell,
But I lived there so merrily, so merrily alone
In the valley of Juab, though Springville's my home.

61. *My House*

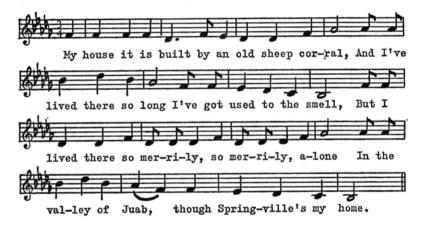

ᎧᏍᎦ 62. *Pleasant Valley* ᎧᏍᎦ

Although this song came from Arizona, it deals with wagon-freighting to Heber Valley, about fifty miles northeast of Salt Lake City. The presentation of the local-color picture of a phase of living which has gone and the use of common language of the workmen make it a significant song.

From the collection of Lenn Shumway of Taylor, Arizona.

Text composed by Lafe Jennings.
Sung by Wilford and Stanley Shumway, Taylor, Arizona, in 1957 for Lenn Shumway.

When you go to Pleasant Valley,
You take a sudden sally
And out through Heber you go.
If you got a big load,
You better take the ridge road,
For the canyon is sandy and slow.
When you get to Nelson's quarters,
You had better go and water,
For your horses will be dry.
Take a bucket and a rope
Down a little rocky slope,
For that is the nearest water by.

Chorus:
Look away, peek away,
To see which way for to go.
If you don't keep a watchin',
It'll be a great caution
If you don't break down the wagon-o.

When you get to the rim,
It'll take a little vim,
For you scarcely can see the ground.
Little boulders are so thick
They will nearly make you sick
And your head will go buzzing around.
Keep your leaders in the track
And hold your wheelers back
And guide them safely through the stumps.

62. *Pleasant Valley*

When you go to Pleas-ant Val-ley, You take a sud-den sal-ly
And out through He - ber you go. If you got a big load,
You bet-ter take the ridge road, For the can-yon is sand-y
and slow. When you get to Nel-son's quar-ters, You had
bet - ter go and wa - ter, For your hors - es
will be dry. Take a buck - et and a rope Down a
lit-tle rock-y slope, For that is the near-est wa-ter by.
CHORUS:
Look a-way, Peek a-way, To see which way for to go. If you
don't keep a watch-in', It'-ll be a great cau-tion If you
don't break down the wag-on-o.

If you hit 'em on the back
It'll make your wheels crack
And you're apt to give your head a little bump.
When you get to Cherry Creek,
If you look right quick

Perhaps you'll see some cherries floating down.
The reason the water's so clear
Is because there's none near,
And you wade across upon the dry ground.
When you go down the mountain,
You'll see a little fountain
Running down the wash so clear;
And a half a hundred hitches
Makes 'em pull like sons-a-bitches,
And to Ellisons' you are near.

When you get to the gate,
You can hardly wait
To get started home again.
You find your wagon light
Before you're back out of sight,
For you're not overstocked with hay and grain.
If you come by Raymond's Ranch
There is only half a chance
For a man to think about his life.
For half the time he's slidin'
And the other half a-glidin'
And to stay with the wagon is a strife.

৩ৡ৹ 63. *Blue Mountain* ৩ৡ৹

Singers like this song, for western strength and vigor mark the tone in every line. The Texan with a questionable past loves Blue Mountain near Monticello in southern Utah, and he loves to dance with the Mormon girls.

It was first contributed by the composer, Judge F. W. Keller, Monticello, Utah (now in Price, Utah), to the Fifes in 1947.

Collected from the composer by Bob Christmas.
Sung by Bob Christmas, Provo, Utah, January 11, 1960.
Other sources: 42 Fife 336; 68 Fife MC I, 608 (Loyal Bailey, Monticello, Utah, 1947); four other entries in the Fife Collection; 71 Sorrels and Fife.

63. *Blue Mountain*

My home it was in Tex-as,   My past you must not know,
I seek a ref-uge from the law Where the sage and piñ-on grow.
CHORUS: Blue Moun-tain you're az - ure deep,   Blue
Moun-tain with sides so steep,   Blue Moun-tain with
horse head on your side, You have won my heart for to keep.

My home it was in Texas,
My past you must not know,
I seek a refuge from the law
Where the sage and the piñon grow.

Chorus:
Blue Mountain you're azure deep,
Blue Mountain with sides so steep,
Blue Mountain with horse head on your side,
You have won my heart for to keep.

I chum with Lattigo Gordon,
I drink at the Blue Goose Saloon,
I dance at night with the Mormon girls
And ride home beneath the moon.

I trade at Mons's store
With the bullet holes in the door.
His calico treasure my horse can measure
When I'm drunk and feeling sore.

Yarn Gallas with shortened bale,
Doc Fewclothes without any soap
In the little green valley have made their sally,
And for the sick there's still some hope.

In the summer the wind doth whine,
In the winter the sun doth shine,
But say, dear brother, if you want a mother
There's Ev on the old chuck line.

64. *Oh Timpanogas, Mighty Timpanogas*

Professor Harrison R. Merrill of Brigham Young University
loved the grand old mountain Timpanogas, the highest of the Wasatch range near Provo, Utah. A great supporter of the annual hike,
he never missed going to the mountain's top, although when I met
him he was in later middle age with well over two hundred pounds
of weight to carry. This song was often sung on the hike. Professor
Merrill would begin it and the other hikers would join in. He wrote
a poem about these mountains, part of which is:

Oh God, let this be heaven,
I do not ask for angel wings,
Just leave that old peak there
And let me climb till comes the night,
I want no golden stair . . .

64. *Oh Timpanogas, Mighty Timpanogas*

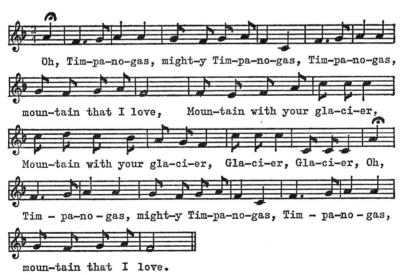

Oh, Tim-pa-no-gas, might-y Tim-pa-no-gas, Tim-pa-no-gas,

moun-tain that I love, Moun-tain with your gla-ci-er,

Moun-tain with your gla-ci-er, Gla-ci-er, Gla-ci-er, Oh,

Tim - pa-no - gas, might-y Tim-pa-no-gas, Tim - pa-no - gas,

moun-tain that I love.

I learned this song from professor Merrill and a group of Timpanogas hikers, while climbing the mountain in 1927.

Oh, Timpanogas, mighty Timpanogas,
Timpanogas, mountain that I love,
Mountain with your glacier,
Mountain with your glacier,
Glacier, Glacier,
Oh, Timpanogas, mighty Timpanogas,
Timpanogas, mountain that I love.

Mountain with your waterfall.

Mountain with your emerald lake.

Mountain with your flowers rare.

Mountain with your cave and heart.

Mountain with your handsome boys.

Mountain with your pretty girls.[1]

☙ 65. *Teton Peaks* ☙

Teton Basin is a small valley about ten by twenty miles in dimension nestled in the mountains of southeastern Idaho. About twenty-five miles to the east over the mountain pass is Jackson, Wyoming, in former times called Jackson's Hole. The composer of this song is unknown, but the people he referred to are not. Mike Yokel was from Jackson's Hole, and in the first decade of the twentieth century he was known in the West for his wrestling prowess. President Driggs, about the same time, was the head official of the Mormon Church in that area, Stake President. The people of the area were chiefly Mormon in religion and the Stake President may very well have had authority and power to influence action of those he found in sin.

Contributed by George Smith, Teton, Idaho, 1932.

---

[1] This song can go on *ad infinitum* with various members of the group contributing new verses.

65. *Teton Peaks*

I came to this land with a gun in my hand To live where there's no-thing to fear. In old Te-ton Bas-in I chose to re-main And make a be-gin-ning from here.

CHORUS: To the east are the Te - ton Peaks Steal-ing my heart from me, Catch-ing the sun on their snow-y tops And turn-ing the blue to gray. Te - tons, Alps of the West, you are the best, I take my rest in your pres - ence, Moun-tains so high, Rock-y Moun-tains and Te - ton Peaks.

I came to this land with a gun in my hand
To live where there's nothing to fear.
In old Teton Basin I chose to remain
And make a beginning from here.

Chorus:
To the east are the Teton Peaks
Stealing my heart from me,
Catching the sun on their snowy tops
And turning the blue to gray.
Tetons, Alps of the West, you are the best,
I take my rest in your presence,

Mountains so high,
Rocky Mountains and Teton Peaks.

I wrestled Mike Yokel one day on the mat,
He put a full nelson on me,
And he said, "You are strong, but you can't get along
With an old Teton wrestler like me."

President Driggs called me in when he found me in sin,
Said, "This thing should not ever be;
You will straighten out if you stay here about,
This is the end of your spree."

CHAPTER IV

Mormon Customs and Teachings

Richard M. Dorson places the Mormons of Utah as one of the four "richest regional folk-cultures of the United States." He wrote of the Mormons: "Alone among American regional groups, the Mormons have developed much of their folklore from stirring events in American history," and goes on to say:

> Mormons sprang into being on American soil before the astonished gaze of the American public, fought bloodily with their neighbors and the federal government, and trekked dramatically westward across the continent in their search for Zion.
>
> An original theology and a new-found church gave the Mormons unity and strength and marked them as a people apart.[1]

Being a people apart, as Dorson says, to some extent made them a "peculiar" people whose customs and teachings are significantly different, as has been shown in previous chapters. The first two songs in this section point out teachings and customs that are specifically Mormon. The many other songs dealing with eating, drinking, fashions, courtship, marriage, thrift, service, church attendance, kindliness, and following the teachings of Jesus, however, show Mormon interests which have parallels elsewhere. Indeed, many customs and teachings presented here are to some extent universal. Although Mormons have sung these songs, some of them are not exclusively Mormon. They are given here because Mormons sing them and claim them for their own, and students of the culture can readily see Mormon local color in every song.

Didacticism is paramount in many of these songs. In any era the dominant characteristics of the literature do not completely submerge other tendencies. Naturalism and symbolism have not completely killed romantic and Victorian tendencies, especially in the

---

[1] Richard M. Dorson, *American Folklore*, p. 113.

Mormon society. The folksinging Mormons are not averse to preaching and to using song, poetry, and story as vehicles for moral teaching. Though they may not express it in a philosophy, they believe that literature to be good must have moral purpose. They cling tenaciously to mid-Victorian concepts. Edgar A. Guest's verse, with its homespun philosophy and its emphatic and sentimental didacticism, is often quoted in church services.

The interest in moral purpose and willingness to preach and be preached to is emphatically demonstrated in the songs in this category.

☜ 66. *None Can Preach the Gospel* ☜
like the Mormons Do

Young missionaries go into the "field" equipped with authority, having been ordained into the Melchizedek Priesthood, and with a "testimony" of the truthfulness of their message, a legacy inherited through the system. Thus they preach the Gospel with conviction and forcefulness rather than with logic or from a background of scholarly training. Truly, "none can preach the Gospel like the Mormons do."

Sung by Karen Woodward, Salt Lake City, Utah, November, 1959.

Other sources: 68 Fife MC I, 673 (Mrs. Mary Hafen Leavitt, St. George, Utah, 1947); 71 Sorrels and Fife; the Fifes have another listing.

> We're going to preach the Gospel
> To all who want to hear.
> A message of salvation
> Unto the meek we'll bear.
> Jehovah has commanded us
> And therefore we must go,
> For none can preach the Gospel
> Like the Mormons do,
> Like the Mormons do.

66. *None Can Preach the Gospel Like the Mormons Do*

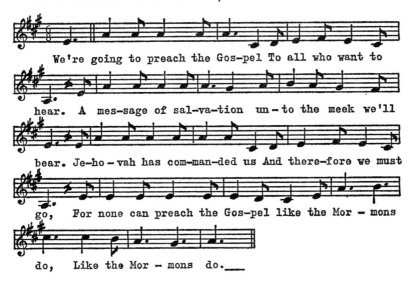

We're going to preach the Gos-pel To all who want to
hear. A mes-sage of sal-va-tion un-to the meek we'll
bear. Je-ho-vah has com-man-ded us And there-fore we must
go, For none can preach the Gos-pel like the Mor-mons
do, Like the Mor-mons do.___

Faith in God and Jesus
Is the first thing that we preach.
Genuine repentance is the next thing
That we teach.
Baptism by immersion
Is the next thing
That we show,
For none can preach the Gospel
Like the Mormons do,
Like the Mormons do.

Two stanzas in addition were presented to the Fifes by Mary
Hafen Leavitt of Utah's Dixie.

Text from leaflet accompanying record, 27 Fife (Side 1, Band 1).

How to obtain the spirit, the next thing that we say,
As in the days of Peter the same as in our day,
'Tis by the laying on of hands and, Oh, we know 'tis true.
That none can preach the gospel like the Mormons do,
  like the Mormons do.

The old-time religion is what we want, you know
With prophets and apostles as in days of long ago.
Read Ezekiel's second chapter, Ephesians four and two.
For none can preach the gospel like the Mormons do,
    like the Mormons do.

67. A Church without a Prophet

The Church maintains missionaries scattered throughout the world proselyting for the Church. One of the first lessons these missionaries give to anyone who will listen is that taught in this song. They maintain with vigor that the modern Church is founded on revelation, that the Church must have a prophet and apostles. The thousands of visitors to the Mormon pavilion in the New York World's Fair of 1964–1965 heard this teaching presented emphatically.

Text from Levette Davidson "Mormon Songs," Journal of American Folklore, *LVIII (October–December, 1945) 275.*[2]

A church without a prophet is not the church for me;
It has no head to lead it, in it I would not be;
    But I've a church not built by man,
    Out from the mountain without hand,
A church with gifts and blessings, oh, that's the church for
    me,
Oh, that's the church for me, oh, that's the church for me.

The God that others worship is not the God for me;
He has no parts nor body, and cannot hear nor see;
    But I've a God that lives above,
    A God of Power and of Love,
A God of Revelation, oh, that's the God for me.

---

[2] Davidson says that the song was sung to the tune of "The Rose that All Are Praising" and that he got it from *History of the Mormons* (Auburn, 1852), pp. 56–61. He also indicated that it appears in *Pioneer Songs* (p. 313) and *Deseret Sunday School Songs* (1909, No. 102), but these last two items are wrong. The song in these listings is "We Thank Thee, Oh God, for a Prophet," a Mormon hymn differing greatly from this song.

A church without apostles is not the church for me;
It's like a ship dismasted afloat upon the sea;
    But I've a church that's always led
    By the twelve stars around its head,
A church with good foundations, oh, that's the church
    for me.

The hope that Gentiles cherish is not the hope for me;
It has no hope for knowledge, far from it I would be;
    But I've a hope that will not fail,
    That reaches safe within the veil,
Which hope is like an anchor, oh, that's the hope for me.

68. *Carrot Greens*

Sanpete County in south-central Utah has been called Carrot
County by the folk, an appelative derived from a tradition of the
pioneers' having survived in early days on carrots. For a change,
they ate carrot greens—and even the cows and horses avoided carrot
tops.

The song is one of the most delightful of folksongs once popular
in southern Utah. Outside Mormon country it is known as "Turnip
Greens."

*Text contributed by Karen Woodward, Salt Lake City, Utah,
November, 1929.*

Other source: 35 Davidson 295.

> The other night I had a dream,
> I dreamt that I could fly,
> I flapped my wings like a buzzard
> And I flew into the sky.
> And there I met St. Peter,
> I met him at the gate.
> He asked me in to dine with him
> And this is what we ate:
>
> *Chorus:*
> Oh—carrot greens,
> Good old carrot greens,

Corn bread and butter milk
And good old carrot greens.

The other night I had a dream,
I dreamt that I had died;
I flapped my wings like an eagle,
And flew into the skies.
And there I saw Moroni,
A-sitting on a spire;
He asked me up and said we'd sup
On this most humble fare:

69. Oh, Touch Not the Wine Cup

Revelation in the Mormon *Doctrine and Covenants*, Section 89,
demands total abstinence from use of intoxicating liquor. The
three songs following deal with drinking; the first two are sentimental songs derived from non-Mormon sources and from the mid-
Victorian era which produced "The Dunkard's Lone Child."

*The original words of this song were written by J. H. Aikman
and, with music by T. H. Bailey, published in* Franklin Square Song
Collection, *III (1885), 78.*
Sung by Don Wakefield, Huntington, Utah, July 2, 1959.

Oh, touch not the wine cup, dear brother, I pray,
Though it gleams in its crystal so bright.
I know you've been thinking of Mother today
And the letter she wrote us last night.
I know that she wept when she wrote to her boys,
For I noticed a blot on each line.
Come home with me, then, for her sake, brother dear,
And taste not, oh, touch not the wine.

Chorus:
Rosy wine, rosy wine, 'round the dear heart to cling like
    a vine;
For 'twill wither and sear all that's bright, brother dear.
Then taste not, oh, touch not the wine.

69. *Oh, Touch Not the Wine Cup*

Oh, touch not the wine cup, dear broth-er, I pray, Though it
gleams in its crys-tal so bright. I know you've been
think-ing of Moth-er to-day And the let-ter she wrote us last
night. I know that she wept when she wrote to her boys,
For I no-ticed a blot on each line. Come home with me, then,
for her sake, broth-er dear, And taste not, oh, touch not the
wine.

CHORUS:

Ros-y wine, ros-y wine, 'round the dear heart to
cling like a vine; For 'twill with-er and sear all that's
bright, broth-er dear. Then taste not, oh, touch not the wine.

Remember our father who fell in the strife,
When the battle was raging so strong.
The last words he uttered was, "God bless my wife,
And protect my brave sons from all harm."
How our dear mother clung to us, then, in her grief,
As we promised her comfort to be;
Come home with me, then, for her sake, brother dear,
And turn from temptation with me.

Oh, touch not the wine cup, dear brother, I pray,
Though it gleams in its crystal so cold,
Like a fire it will burn at your heart strings, and blight
All the good resolutions of old.
Dash it down, 'tis a thing to be dreaded and shunned,
And go write to our mother a line.
How, though tempted, we'll strive, for her sake, brother dear,
We have manfully turned from the wine.

70. Have Courage, My Boy, To Say No!

In Mormon church services in my youth I often heard speakers plead with the people to "keep the Word of Wisdom," which meant to refrain from use of four items designated in the document as harmful to the body—tea, coffee, tobacco, and alcoholic beverages. In admonishing people to refrain from use of "strong drink," speakers in church and teachers in church auxiliary organizations often used a sentimental approach like that used in this song. When Mr. Hilton sang it for me, I remembered specific lines and the offensive didacticism of the method of presenting the message.

Sung by L. M. Hilton, Ogden, Utah, October, 1959.

You've started today on life's journey
Alone on the highway of life,
You'll meet with a thousand temptations,
Each city with evil is rife,
The world is a stage of excitement
No matter wherever you go.
But if you are tempted in weakness,
Have courage, my boy, to say no.

Chorus:
Have courage, my boy, to say no,
Have courage, my boy, to say no,
Have courage, my boy, have courage, my boy,
Have courage, my boy, to say no!

The bright ruby wine may be offered,
No matter how tempting it be,

70. *Have Courage, My Boy, To Say No!*

You've start-ed to-day on life's jour-ney A-lone on the high-way of life, You'll meet with a thou-sand temp-ta-tions, Each cit-y with e-vil is rife, The world is a stage of ex-cite-ment No mat-ter wher-ev-er you go, But if you are tempt-ed in weak-ness, Have cour-age, my boy, to say no.

CHORUS: Have cour-age, my boy, to say no, Have cour-age, my boy, to say no, Have cour-age, my boy, have cour-age, my boy, Have cour-age, my boy, to say no!

From poison that stings like a viper
Have courage, my boy, to flee.
The vile gambling dens are before you,
The lights how they dance to and fro,
But if you are tempted to enter,
Have courage, my boy, to say no.

In courage alone lies your safety
When you the lone journey begin,
But trust in your Heavenly Father
Will keep you unspotted from sin.

Temptations will keep on increasing
Like streams from a rivulet flow,
But if you are true to your manhood,
Have courage, my boy, to say no.

ᏸ 71. *Be Home Early Tonight, My Dear Boy* ᏸ

This preachy song with its tear-jerking homily on evils of
gambling and drink is offensive in its saccharine sentimentality; yet
good people savored it a generation or two ago both in and out of
Mormon country. My mother sang it to her children; I remember
hearing it about 1912, when we lived in southeastern Idaho where
life was vigorous, men were tough, and drinking and gambling men
were well known.

In 1933, I collected a version of this song from Mrs. R. F. Wanless
of Victor, Idaho. The version appearing here is from M. E. Wakefield.

Sung by M. E. Wakefield, Ogden, Utah, July 27, 1958.

I've traveled through life and I've seen many things
To surprise me in every form.
I've been at the plow and I've been at the spade
From daylight, to sunrise, to the morn.
Then at night when I'd go for some pleasure in town—
It was always for pleasure and joy—
My mother would say when going away,
"Be home early tonight, my dear boy."

Chorus:
"Be home early tonight, my dear boy,
Be home early tonight, my dear boy;
Don't spend all your money in gamble and drink,
Be home early tonight, my dear boy."

One night I left home when my poor mother was sick
With a fever of torture and pain.
Said she, "My dear boy, take this message I give
I may never give you it again."
And when I returned from my night's fun and joy,

71. *Be Home Early Tonight, My Dear Boy*

I've trav-eled through life and I've seen man-y things To sur-prise me in ev - ery form. I've been at the plow and I've been at the spade From day-light, to sun-rise, to the morn. Then at night when I'd go for some pleas-ure in town— It was al-ways for pleas-ure and joy— My moth-er would say when go-ing a-way, "Be home ear-ly to-night, my dear boy."

CHORUS:

"Be home ear-ly to-night, my dear boy, Be home ear-ly to-night, my dear boy; Don't spend all your mon-ey in gam-ble and drink, Be home ear-ly to-night, my dear boy."

I heard my dear mother was dead.
'Twas then a cold chill through my body did run
As I thought of the last words she said:

Young men, let me give you one piece of advice,
To your father and mother attend.

A good mother's love it should not be forgot;
When she's dead you have lost your best friend.
Don't spend all your money in gamble and drink,
For there's many a thing to enjoy;
Take this motto I give, 'twas a mother's request,
"Keep good hours at night, my dear boy."

☙ 72. *The Good Old Keg of Wine* ❧

Of Mormon origin, this is a jolly drinking song with a Tam-o-
Shanter touch of joyful exuberance. Yet at the same time it shows in
mild satire the evil results of getting "boozy woozy."

Composed by Moses E. Gifford.
Contributed by Lillian Christensen, descendant of the author, in
1960.
Other source: 68 Fife MC I, 774 (Carl Gifford, son of Moses
Gifford, St. George, Utah, 1947).
Tune: "The Good Old Summer Time."

There's a time in each year when the boys do feel queer
With the good old keg of wine;
Like birds of a feather, they all flock together
Where the sun refuses to shine;
Forgetting their sorrow, no trouble they borrow,
When giddy they think it is fine.
Their neighbors annoying, themselves are enjoying
The good old keg of wine.

Chorus:
The good old keg of wine, boys, now don't you look fine
Strolling up and down the street, singing keggy mine;
I'll hold your head, the keg holds mine, and that's a very
   good sign
That they got boozy woozy on the good old keg of wine.

When the weather is warm, like bees that will swarm
With the good old keg of wine,
And when it is cold, a wife she will scold
At the good old keg of wine,

When the stomach grows sour, they'll heave for an hour;
When called to a meal, they'll decline;
They try not to show it, think the women don't know it,
With the good old keg of wine.

Chorus:
The good old keg of wine, boys, now don't you look fine
Sprawling out upon the ground, singing keggy mine,
I'll hold your head, the ground bumped mine, and that's a
　very good sign
That they got boozy woozy on the good old keg of wine.

They gather in groups, go out to hen coops
With the good old keg of wine;
Their deeds are not mean, they're heard but not seen,
With the good old keg of wine;
In the pig pen they tumble, they don't seem to grumble
When rooting around with the swine; they think they're
　advancing,
Hog music for dancing, with the good old keg of wine.

⟡ 73. *Ditches Break Again No More* ⟡

Settlers had had no experience with irrigation when they began
building ditches and flooding land in the mountain valleys. The
ditch banks breaking and the water escaping was a threat to crops
and to food supply. This song is light in tone and covers two subjects,
the second one being a memory of long dresses the pioneer women
wore.

Composed by Moses E. Gifford.
Contributed by Lillian Christensen, Provo, Utah, November,
1960.
Tune: "Hard Times Come Again No More."

Oh, how well do I remember, when thoughts of bygone days—
How those memories are bringing ever near,
When I sit and muse and ponder, I feel somewhat amazed
As those memories are ringing in my ears.

'Tis the song and the prayer of the people:
Ditches, ditches, break again no more;
Many times we have mended places in which you broke before.
O, ditches break that way no more.

I remember when my father, returning home at night,
And my mother greets him at the door;
I can see her old long dresses a dragging on the floor;
O, dresses, drag that way no more.

You can see my mother old and weary,
With her dresses dragging on the floor;
Many days she dragged those dresses 'round the cabin door;
O, dresses, drag that way no more.

74. A Burlesque on the
Fashions of the Day, 1870
or
The Grecian Bend

In 1967, a "Beatle haircut," a hair trim and styling for men which
makes the hair look like a cap over the head and eyes, is the subject
for satire and the target for wit. In Utah in 1870, bustles held the
spotlight. Charles Walker, composer of this song, saw an opportunity to fire his dart at a popular fad in dress.

*Composed by Charles L. Walker and copied from his journal, in
possession of Kathryn M. Larson, St. George, Utah, May 17, 1960.
Sung by Elayne Clark, Provo, Utah, June 27, 1962.*

> Come all ye gents and ladies
> And listen to my rhyme
> While I relate a song to you
> To pass away the time.
> It's of the modern fashions
> That seem to have no end,
> And the latest one that's all the rage
> Is this stylish Grecian bend.

74. *A Burlesque on the Fashions of the Day, 1870*

or

The Grecian Bend

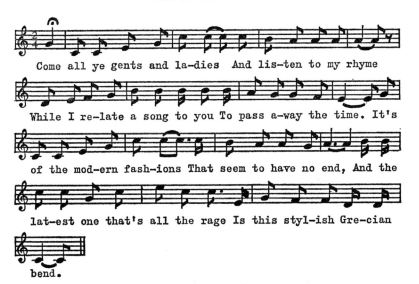

Come all ye gents and la-dies And lis-ten to my rhyme

While I re-late a song to you To pass a-way the time. It's

of the mod-ern fash-ions That seem to have no end, And the

lat-est one that's all the rage Is this styl-ish Gre-cian

bend.

When dame nature first made women,
She turned them out complete
Without a waterfall behind
Or high heels on their feet.
They were well made, plump and beautiful,
And straight from end to end
Without that hard, hard hump behind
Now styled the Grecian bend.

In the good old times a lady
Counted ringlets no disgrace
As they hung in rich profusion
Round about her pretty face;
Now they shingle, crop and frizzle
It in styles that have no end
And stick it out a way behind
Just like the Grecian bend.

I see the hump with sorrow
As they promenade the road
Strapped on with bows and britchen
Like a pack mule with a load.
They try to make the human
And the dromedary blend
By sticking out a hump behind
They call the Grecian bend.

The next new fashion we receive
From New York by the mail
Will be splice out your Grecian bend
And attach it to a tail.
A black cow's tail will be prepared
With the bush hacked off the end
To make the last improvement
On this horrid Grecian bend.

Next fashion that we get from France
When belles go out-of-doors,
Just slightly stoop upon the ground
And go it on all fours.
Then fix a carrot on your head
With a sunflower on the end
And tie a cowboy along the hump,
The stylish Grecian bend.

ᏋᎧ 75. Sparking Sunday Night ᏋᎧ

Although I could not get this song from Job Porter of Victor, Idaho, I remember his singing it when I was a child. In pioneer celebrations in that Mormon community his singing of the song was in popular demand. An interesting name for courtship, the word "sparking" had spicy connotations and was much in vogue, as were the related words "bundling" and "spooning" in and out of Mormon country. The reference in the song to "things the folks in meeting said" fits well into Mormon life, although reference to the minister is certainly not Mormon. The song is among those the Mormons got from elsewhere and made their own.

Sung by Karen Woodward, Salt Lake City, Utah, November, 1959.
Other source: 39 Durham 305.

75. *Sparking Sunday Night*

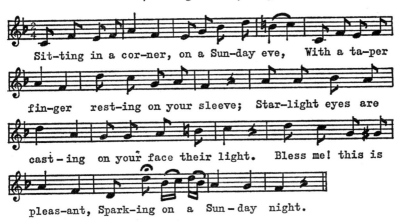

Sitting in a corner, on a Sunday eve,
With a taper finger resting on your sleeve;
Starlight eyes are casting on your face their light.
Bless me! this is pleasant, sparking on a Sunday night.

How your heart is thumping 'gainst your Sunday vest,
How wickedly 'tis working on this day of rest.
Hours seem but minutes as they take their flight.
Bless me! ain't this pleasant, sparking on a Sunday night.

Dad and Marm are sleeping in their peaceful bed,
Dreaming of the things the folks in meeting said.
"Love ye one another," Ministers recite.
Bless me! don't we do it sparking on a Sunday night.

One arm with gentle pressure lingers round her waist,
You squeeze her dimpled hand, her pouting lips you taste.
She freely slaps your face, but more in love than spite.
Thunder! ain't it pleasant, sparking on a Sunday night.

But hark! the clock is striking, it's two o'clock I sum.
Sure as I'm a sinner, th' time to go has come.

You ask in spiteful accents if that old clock is right?
And wonder if it ever sparked on a Sunday night.

One, two, three, sweet kisses, four five, six you hook;
But, thinking that you rob her, put back those you took;
Then, as for home you hurry from the fair one's sight.
Oh, but don't you wish each was only Sunday night.

76. Julius Hannig's Wedding

This song and the one following were contributed by Karl Larson
of St. George, Utah. He says each song commemorates a wedding of
the early days in the town of Washington, Utah, about ten miles
north of St. George. The names and incidents are all accurate, according to the collector, a historian and folklorist vitally interested
in customs of the early Mormon people. His book *The Red Hills of
November* gives more details of the courtship and marriage customs
in Washington than we find in these songs; yet, getting the wine in
the Mormon community, getting the groom to give a dance, the
shivaree—all reveal customs any folklorist finds interesting.

Composed by Rube Jolley.
Sung by Andrew Karl Larson, St. George, Utah, April 17, 1960.

Now white folks, your attention, and I'll sing to you a song
About Julius Hannig's wedding, and it won't detain you long.
He's been a-getting married now for six or seven years,
But he couldn't get the girl's consent till April did appear.

Now when he got the girl's consent, why he began to prance;
He went and got a keg of wine, but he wouldn't give a dance.
The boys they thought it pretty good, and Julius thought it fine,
So they all went up to Boggs's, and you bet they had a time!

Now where they got that keg of wine, this is just what played
    hell,
They fixed it so the boys, they could neither drink nor smell.
They fined Old Mac so very high, they thought they'd done
    him well,
But all the boys in Washington wished Paxman was in hell!

76. *Julius Hannig's Wedding*

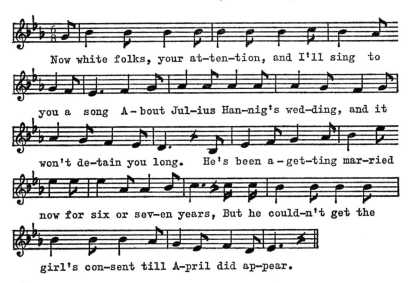

Now white folks, your at-ten-tion, and I'll sing to
you a song A-bout Jul-ius Han-nig's wed-ding, and it
won't de-tain you long. He's been a-get-ting mar-ried
now for six or sev-en years, But he could-n't get the
girl's con-sent till A-pril did ap-pear.

Ed Van Orden is the Mayor, and of course you all know that
He always prowls around the town just like an old stray cat.
I think he'd better stay at home or else down to the store,
For there he has a plenty o' clothes and don't need any more.

Randolph Andrus is the marshal and he's got a brand new hat,
He wears a white silk handkerchief, likewise a new cravat;
He has a pair of brand new pants to ornament his frame;
You bet he'll trig himself right up if he gets back again.

If you want a drink of wine, boys, you mustn't go to Mac
Nor to Old Lady Larson, for they'll say to you, "Go back!
Forty dollars is too much to pay for every little fine
For selling boys on wedding days a little keg of wine!"

77. Charlie Knell's Wedding

Sung by Andrew Karl Larson, St. George, Utah, April 17, 1960.

77. Charlie Knell's Wedding

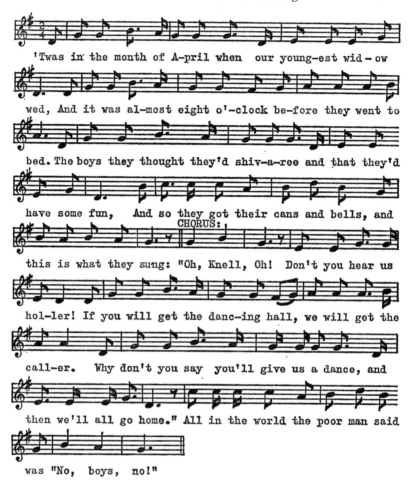

'Twas in the month of A-pril when our young-est wid-ow wed, And it was al-most eight o'-clock be-fore they went to bed. The boys they thought they'd shiv-a-ree and that they'd have some fun, And so they got their cans and bells, and this is what they sung: "Oh, Knell, Oh! Don't you hear us hol-ler! If you will get the danc-ing hall, we will get the call-er. Why don't you say you'll give us a dance, and then we'll all go home." All in the world the poor man said was "No, boys, no!"

'Twas in the month of April when our youngest widow wed,
And it was almost eight o'clock before they went to bed.
The boys, they thought they'd shivaree and that they'd have
    some fun,

And so they got their cans and bells, and this is what they
    sung:

Chorus:
"Oh, Knell, Oh! Don't you hear us holler!
If you will get the dancing hall, we will get the caller.
Why don't you say you'll give us a dance, and then we'll
    all go home,"
All in the world the poor man said was, "No, Boys, no!"

We went upon the doorstep then and played our music sweet;
Knellie came out into the door all in his stocking feet.
He said, "Now, Boys, I'm much obliged, I tell you that was fine!"
And then the boys, they all yelled out, "Why don't you get
    the wine?"

The old lady gave it up right there, and she went back to bed,
And Frankie Barron, he slept so sound, they thought that he
    was dead.
Huldy, she of course was mad, and this is what she said,
"I wish them bells were all in hell and all the boys were dead!"

78. *The Loafer's Lament*

A complaint on coming to one's last greenback is not uncommon
in any society, but this typical, mildly satirical lament came from
the local poet of Utah's Dixie in 1864.

*Composed by Charles L. Walker and copied from his journal, in
possession of Kathryn M. Larson, St. George, Utah, April 17, 1960.
Tune: "The Last Rose of Summer."*

'Tis the last greenback dollar left crumpled alone,
    All the fives, tens, and twenties are gambled and gone,
    No note of its kindred, no specie is nigh,
    And I'm broke for sartin and heave sigh for sigh.

I'll not leave thee, thou loved one, to wear out alone,
    Since thy mates are all missing, thou too must be gone.
    Thus kindly I stow thee away in my purse
    To pay for a toddy or perhaps something worse.

Oh, soon may I follow, when greenbacks won't stay,
And Ike's silver dollars are squandered away,
When greenbacks have vanished and specie has flown,
Oh, who would inhabit this hard world alone.

☙ 79. *Waste Not, Want Not* ❧

A book could be written on the many economies practiced by the pioneers who despite their rigid habits of thrift were forced to live in abject poverty. In the spirit of "Waste Not, Want Not," Mormon settlers in the West saved the first dishwater to feed the pigs, made jam out of fruit peelings and watermelon rinds, made quilts out of the best parts of worn-out clothing, made soap from waste fat, polished shoes with stove black, and practiced a thousand other economies not known in modern America. This didactic song is one Mormons liked and sang. Don Wakefield, who said he "used to sing it," also said that his parents of Huntington, Utah, sang it hundreds of times in the gatherings.

Sung by Don Wakefield, Huntington, Utah, 1958.
Other sources: 39 Durham 96; 68 Fife MC I, 588 (Joseph H. Watkins, Brigham City, Utah, 1946).

When a child I lived at Lincoln with my parents on the farm,
The lessons that my mother taught to me were quite a charm;
She would often take me on her knee when tired of childish play,
And as she pressed me to her breast, I've heard my mother say:

Chorus:
Waste not, want not, is the maxim I would teach.
Let your watchword be dispatch, and practice what you preach;
Do not let your chances like sunbeams pass you by,
For you never miss the water till the well runs dry.

As years rolled on I grew to be a mischief-making boy,
Destruction seemed my only sport, it was my only joy;
And well do I remember, when oft-times well chastised,
How father sat beside me then, and thus had me advised:

79. *Waste Not, Want Not*

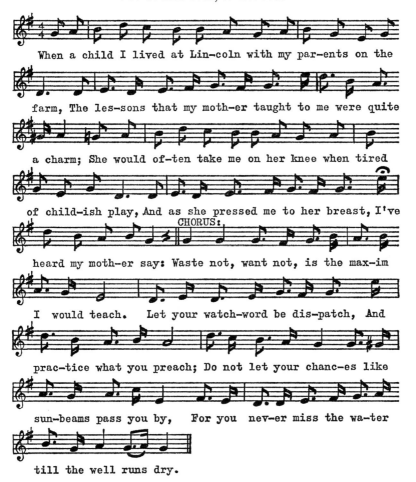

When a child I lived at Lin-coln with my par-ents on the

farm, The les-sons that my moth-er taught to me were quite

a charm; She would of-ten take me on her knee when tired

of child-ish play, And as she pressed me to her breast, I've

heard my moth-er say: Waste not, want not, is the max-im

I would teach. Let your watch-word be dis-patch, And

prac-tice what you preach; Do not let your chanc-es like

sun-beams pass you by, For you nev-er miss the wa-ter

till the well runs dry.

When I arrived at manhood I embarked in public life,
And found it was a rugged road, bestrewn with care and strife;
I speculated foolishly, my losses were severe,
But still a tiny little voice kept whisp'ring in my ear:

Then I studied strict economy, and found to my surprise,
My funds instead of sinking very quickly then did rise;

I grasped each chance and always struck the iron while 'twas hot,
I seized my opportunities, and never once forgot:

I'm married now and happy, I've a careful little wife,
We live in peace and harmony, devoid of care and strife;
Kind fortune smiles upon us, we have little children three,
The lessons that I teach them, as they prattle round my knee:

80. Cold Winter Is Coming

A short version of this song is in the possession of Leroy Robertson of Salt Lake City, Utah. He remembers it as a fascinating song his mother sang in Fountain Green, Utah, in his youth. M. E. Wakefield says that his father composed the song about 1870 and that these are original words, but like so many folk informants, Mr. Wakefield was misinformed. The song is widely known outside Mormondom.

Sung by M. E. Wakefield, Ogden, Utah, July 27, 1958.

Cold winter is coming, there's frost in the air,
The beautiful summer is past,
The flowers are all dying that once were so fair,
Their fragrance has gone with the blast.
The tops of the mountains are covered with snow,
The north wind comes under your door;
Then if you are able to pay what you owe,
'Tis time to remember the poor.

Cold winter is coming, his footsteps are near,
He will spread desolation around,
And make the earth dreary, and frosty, and sear,
And scatter the snow o'er the ground.
The leaves have turned yellow and fallen from the trees,
The beautiful harvest is o'er,
The beautiful brooks are beginning to freeze,
'Tis time to remember the poor.

Cold winter is coming, his cold icy breath
Is whistling through mountain and dell,

80. *Cold Winter Is Coming*

Cold win-ter is com-ing, there's frost in the air, The beau-ti-ful sum-mer is past, The flowers are all dy-ing that once were so fair, Their fra-grance has gone with the blast. The tops of the moun-tains are cov-ered with snow, The north wind comes un-der your door; Then if you are a-ble to pay what you owe, 'Tis time to re-mem-ber the poor.

All nature he'll touch with the finger of death
And lock up the earth with his spell.
He will laugh at the needy and mock at the poor
As widely he opens their door;
Then try to spare something, a mite every day
A blessing will seem to the poor.

Cold winter is coming; where plenty abounds
The dance and the song will be heard;
With mirth and with music your halls will resound
And many will bow at your word.
Then remember the poor, let their hearts be made glad
By something you spare from your store;
It will nourish the feeble and cheer up the sad,
So be sure to remember the poor.

81. *Mogos, Nogos, Everybody Come*[3]
(Version of "Old Folks, Young Folks, Everybody Come")

The song "Old Folks, Young Folks, Everybody Come" has truly become the property of the folk. Its delightful, humorous hyperbole is easy to simulate, so it can be revised or supplemented for use on particular occasions. In my collection are nine versions, two of which—this song and the one following—are presented here. These Mormon parodies of an original "Darkies' Sunday School" are used to encourage attendance in church auxiliary organizations. The first of the two is for the Mutual Improvement Association, an organization sponsoring entertainment as well as religious training for young people. The second is used to encourage attendance in Sunday School, and, unlike the original, adapts *Book of Mormon* stories instead of Bible stories to the purpose. Two facts which Mormons would know and which add to the humor and satire in the final verses are that Mahonri, Moriancumer's brother, is a significant character who is never named in the book, and "reformed Egyptian" was the original language in which the *Book of Mormon* was written.

Sung by Ray Decker, Provo, Utah, November, 1959.

The Lord made Satan and Satan made sin;
The Lord made a hot place to put Satan in,
Satan didn't like it and said he wouldn't stay,
And he's been a raisin' Nogos ever since that day.

Chorus:
Mogos, Nogos, everybody come.
Join the 9th Ward M.I.A. and have a lot of fun.
Please check your chewing gum and razors at the door,
And you'll hear some Bible stories that you never heard before.

The earth was made in six days and finished on the seventh;
According to the contract it should have been the eleventh;
The carpenters got drunk and the Nogos wouldn't work,
So all that they could do was fill it up with dirt.

Cain was a Nogo and Abel was a good;
Cain hit his brother with a stick as any brother would.

---

[3] A "Mogo" is a person who goes to Mutual and a "Nogo" is one who does not,

81. *Mogos, Nogos, Everybody Come*

The Lord made Sa-tan and Sa-tan made sin; The Lord made
a hot place to put Sa-tan in. Sa-tan did-n't like it and
said he would-n't stay, And he's been a-rais-in' No-gos ev-er
since that day. *CHORUS:* Mo - gos, No - gos, ev-ery bo-dy come.
Join the 9th Ward M. I. A. and have a lot of fun.
Please check your chew-ing gum and ra-zors at the door,
And you'll hear some Bi-ble sto-ries that you nev-er heard
be-fore.

Abel didn't like it and he asked him to refrain,
But Cain wasn't able so Abel got the cane.

Jonah was a Nogo with a tendency to sail,
He wouldn't come to M.I.A., but rode within a whale.
He didn't like his quarters although they were the best,
So Jonah pushed the button and the whale did the rest.

Sampson was a scrapper for the Cougar wrestling school,
He licked a thousand Utes with the jaw bone of a mule.[4]

[4] The words "Cougar" and "Ute" in these lines about Samson refer to the Brigham Young University and the University of Utah athletic teams, traditional sports foes.

But a Nogo named Delilah filled him full of gin,
Clipped off his whiskers and the Bishop ran him in.

Ruth she was a Nogo of the very modern type,
She wagged a wicked lipstick, and she rode a motor bike.
When she came to B.Y.U. her eye was on the glad,
The M.I.A. saved her from going to the bad.

82. *The Mormon Sunday School Song*

(Version of "Old Folks, Young Folks, Everybody Come")

Contributed by Dennis Flake, October 26, 1964.

The Prophet Nephi was brave and strong
In the scriptures he could do no wrong.
The way Arnold Frieberg painted him
He must have worked out at Steve Reeves' gym.

Chorus:
Young folks, old folks, everybody come,
Join the Mormon Sunday School and have a lot of fun.
Pay your tithing, building fund, and budget at the door
And you'll hear some Scripture stories that you've never
    heard before.

Old King Benjamin built himself a tower
To preach to the folks for many an hour.
They pitched their tents so they could see.
And it looked like a Boy Scout Jamboree.

The Gadianton Robbers get all the thanks
For robbing all of the Nephite banks.
They robbed every bank in the whole damnation,
Because they had the secret combination.

The Ammonites knew what was right,
They did their best to avoid a fight,
But when things got going hard
They called out the National Guard.

They had a little trouble with Alma, the younger,
For spiritual enlightenment he did hunger.
An angel appeared in glorious rays,
He felt sort of dumb for a couple of days.

The Jaredites left the tower of Babel.
They had two leaders who were strong and able.
Mahonri Moriancumer won great fame;
I can't remember his brother's name.

Buy a *Book of Mormon* without delay
Just "four bits" is all you pay.
I'll tell you what it will do:
If it reformed Egyptian, it will reform you!

83. *Thirty Pieces of Silver*

The kernel of the betrayal story as told here may or may not be
derived from the Child ballad (23), though it deals with the same
subject. The Child ballad endows Judas with a sister more perfidious
than himself and provides Judas with a motive for selling his master
not verified in the Scriptures: having been robbed of the silver en-
trusted to him and making what he thought to be a shrewd deal to
recover the lost money, he was motivated by a belief that Christ,
being divine, could not be taken. This is a song which is probably not
Mormon in origin. Its biblical subject matter, however, is com-
monly used in Mormon gatherings.

*Contributed by Kay Senzee, Provo, Utah, 1959. She obtained the
song from her grandparents, who remembered the words but had
forgotten the melody.*

'Tis a sad but true story, from the Bible it came,
And it tells us how Judas sold the Saviour in shame.
He planned with the Council of high priests that day;
Thirty pieces of silver was the price they would pay.

Thirty pieces of silver, thirty shekels of shame,
Was the price paid for Jesus, on the cross He was slain,
Betrayed and forsaken, unloved and unclaimed.
In anger they pierced Him, but He died not in vain.

'Twas there on the hillside the multitude came
And found our dear Saviour, then took Him away.
They smote and they mocked Him, thorns were crowned
   'round his head,
And the raiment of purple showed the blood stains of red.

Far off in the mountain with face toward the sun
Judas begged mercy for what he had done.
He gave back the silver, for his heart filled with strife,
Then there in the mountains he took his own life.

Thirty pieces of silver, thirty shekels of shame
Was the price paid for Jesus, on the cross He was slain.

༺ 84. *Mottos on the Wall* ༻

Mr. Jesse Jepsen, a seventy-five year old singer from St. George, Utah, says he has never seen this song in print. He learned it, he thinks, from an entertainer who sang it when Jepsen was a youth. The didactic tone, the sentiment of love for home and mother, the portrayal of the old time home with mottos on the wall—all reflect the home life and sentimentality which Utah settlers loved and engendered.

Sung by Jesse Jepsen, April 17, 1960.

There's a wealth of pure affection,
There's a red rose speck of joy
Mingled with my thoughts of Mother and of home.
I've a tender recollection of her teachings when a boy
That seem to hover round where'er I roam.
Now her gentle form reposes 'neath the daisies on the hill
As an offering to Him who loves us all,
And her spirit hovering near
Seems to whisper to me still
From mottos that were framed upon our wall.

Chorus:
"God Bless Our Home," "In God We Trust,"
"Kind Words of Welcome to All,"

84. *Mottos on the Wall*

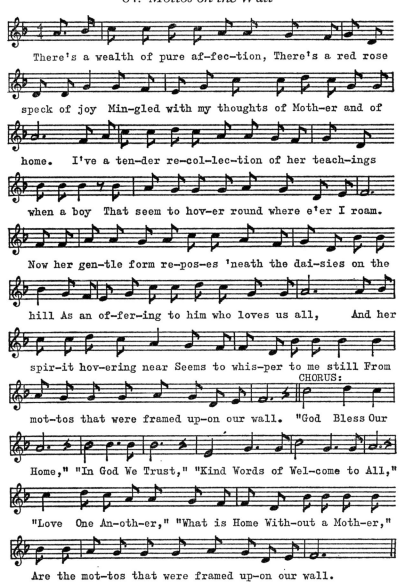

There's a wealth of pure af-fec-tion, There's a red rose
speck of joy Min-gled with my thoughts of Moth-er and of
home. I've a ten-der re-col-lec-tion of her teach-ings
when a boy That seem to hov-er round where e'er I roam.
Now her gen-tle form re-pos-es 'neath the dai-sies on the
hill As an of-fer-ing to him who loves us all, And her
spir-it hov-ering near Seems to whis-per to me still From

CHORUS:

mot-tos that were framed up-on our wall. "God Bless Our
Home," "In God We Trust," "Kind Words of Wel-come to All,"
"Love One An-oth-er," "What is Home With-out a Moth-er,"
Are the mot-tos that were framed up-on our wall.

"Love One Another," "What Is Home Without a Mother,"
Are the mottos that were framed upon our wall.

While kneeling in the evening I have echoed Mother's prayer,
And I've lingered for a gentle, loving kiss.
I have heard her, "Goodnight darling,"
As I climbed upon the stairs.
To me there was no sweeter sound than this.
Every window, every door,
Every nail that's in the floor,
Every crevice from the kitchen to the hall
Are engraven on my heart, and from memory ne'er shall
    part
From the mottos that were framed upon our wall.

Be it ever so humble,
There's no place like home. (Modulation to tune of
    "Home Sweet Home.")

85. The Lifeboat

The singing Wakefields from whom this song came believe that
it was brought home by a missionary who had been in England. It
appears to have had both sailor and Negro influence. The basic
metaphor appeals to singers and the melody fittingly supports the
message. Admonition to "pray night and day" and retain hope "If
you want to sail with Jesus in de lifeboat" squares with Mormon
teaching.

Both Don Wakefield of Huntington, Utah, and his brother, M. E.
Wakefield of Ogden, Utah, gave me this song in 1958.

Sung by Don Wakefield, Huntington, Utah, June 17, 1958.

Come, brudder sailors, and don't you fall asleep,
Pray night and day or you'll sink in de deep.
Hope is de anchor and dis you must keep
If you want to sail with Jesus in de lifeboat.

Chorus:
Let me in de lifeboat, let me in de lifeboat,
She can stand de ragin' storm.

85. *The Lifeboat*

Come, brud-der sail-ors, and don't you fall a-sleep,

Pray night and day or you'll sink in de deep. Hope is de

an-chor and dis you must keep If you want to sail with

Je-sus in de life - boat. Let me in de life-boat,

let me in de life-boat, She can stand de ra-gin' storm.

Let me in de life-boat, let me in de life-boat, She will

bear my spi-rit home.

Let me in de lifeboat, let me in de lifeboat,
She will bear my spirit home.

De storm it is heavy and de wind is very loud,
De thunder am a rollin' and it's bustin' in de cloud.
See ebery sailor standin' at his post
Waitin' for de orders from de lifeboat.

Oh, sail, brudder sailors, de port am very nigh,
Hoist up de sails and we'll soon reach de port.
Fadder, Mudder prayin' so hard,
So take de dyin' sailor in de lifeboat.

CHAPTER V

Satire and Sin

Songs in this chapter are anti-Mormon satire or ballads of historical incidents telling stories of murder or sin. Much of anti-Mormon
satire has been sung by Mormons who see faults in the behavior
patterns of members of their society and take delight in exposing
them. The stories of murder are quite as shocking to the Mormon
folk as to non-Mormons. For that reason, the Mormons have written
song stories of the murders and tragedies within the society.

It is difficult to ascertain the popularity among Mormons of
three of these songs: "Porter Rockwell," "Wheat," and "Mountain
Meadows Massacre." With Mormon people I find that opinions
differ regarding Porter Rockwell. Many people who knew him do
not remember him as the quick-triggered "Terror of the Plains"
who had killed so many men. Mormon historians and folklorists are
interested in him as a folk hero. The song, "Mountain Meadows
Massacre," has been popular with non-Mormons. The cruelty and
injustice of the mass murders are too shameful for Mormons to accept; Mormons disown the members who participated in the massacre rather than accept it as a violent act belonging to their society.

The first ten songs in this group deal with Mormon marriage
customs, and most of them with polygamy. Humorists among
writers, entertainers, and the folk have found polygamy always
good for a laugh. As an object of satire in and out of the Church it
has been under constant fire.

The history of polygamy in the Church in brief was as follows:
In 1852, after the Mormons had found a home in the West, Brigham
Young made a public acknowledgment of the doctrine which had
been instituted in the Church by Joseph Smith before his death.
Brigham Young urged its practice under restriction.

Not every married man could take another wife. He had to first secure permission of the president of the church. For only he, or someone delegated by him, could perform a plural marriage ceremony. Otherwise it was a case of adultery and thus punishable by excommunication. Presumably the candidate for a second wife had the necessary qualifications—physical, mental, moral, spiritual, and financial. That was the theory. Polygamy was therefore limited to those who were "fit."

And then whoever wished to marry in polygamy had next to obtain the "consent" of the wife he already had. If, however, that consent was denied, he was free to do as he pleased in the situation. Usually approval was granted—for reasons the wife probably kept to herself.[1]

The chief reasons given by Church leaders for instituting polygamy are first, to abide by divine command; second, to provide earthly bodies for heavenly spirits;[2] third, to provide all women a chance to marry; and fourth, to prevent prostitution. Church leaders philosophized that every woman had the inherent right to have the privilege of motherhood and that to deny her that right and the right to marital satisfaction was to encourage prostitution.

Polygamy died hard among the Mormons. When Congress passed anti-polygamy laws, the Saints refused to give up their doctrine (see Songs No. 29 and 30). The men preferred to go to jail, and hundreds of them did. Officially the practice was discontinued September 24, 1890, when the President of the Church, Wilford Woodruff, issued the "Manifesto" prohibiting its practice. Since that time, marrying into polygamy by a limited number of dissenters has been a constant stinger touching the nerves of the Church. Joseph Smith had given the command as a revelation with heavenly sanction. Certain dissenting people have from time to time put forth claims that God's will was not followed in the issuing of the "Manifesto." Those who in recent years have married in polygamy and have been apprehended have been promptly excommunicated.

The songs given in this area on polygamy are representative of a mass of satire on the subject. A fragment of a song given by Vardis Fisher goes as follows:

> In the Mormon beds out West,
> There the concubines do rest,
> While their husband visits Emily and Jane!
> Oh, the babies do abound

---

[1] John Henry Evans, *One Hundred Years of Mormonism*, pp. 272–273.

[2] See the discussion of Mormon emphasis on large families and family life on pp. 13–14.

> In tens of thousands all around,
> While the husband now slips in to see Elaine![3]

Another fragment refers to Parley P. Pratt, an apostle in the Church during the presidential tenure of Brigham Young. Pratt, when serving as a missionary in Arkansas, took a divorced woman home and married her as a plural wife. The irate divorced husband hunted the Mormon down and killed him. Following is the admonition to "wife stealers":

> Just let this be a warning to wife-stealers—
> Stay away!
> You cannot come to Arkansas and steal another's wife.
> And if you dare to try it you will surely have to pay.
> Yes! You must pay most dearly with your life.[4]

ᎧᏬ 86. *Brigham, Brigham Young* ᎧᏬ

Contributed by Mrs. Peter Hamblin of Victor, Idaho, September 1932. Mrs. Hamblin said her family used to sing the song in St. George, Utah. Copied from her "keepsake notebook."

Sung by Heber Peterson, Burley, Idaho, 1932, in a shorter version. Other sources: 42 Fife 121–122; 43 Hubbard 408; 53 Lomax 388– 391; 54 Lomax 400–401; 57 Put 53; 68 Fife MC I, 577 (Lydia Watts, Moab, Utah, 1946); two other entries in the Fife Collection.

> Old Brigham Young was a Mormon bold,
>   And a leader of the roaring rams,
> And a shepherd of a heap of pretty little sheep,
>   And a nice fold of pretty little lambs.
> And he lived with five and forty wives
>   In the city of Great Salt Lake
> Where they woo and coo as pretty doves do
>   And cackle like ducks to a drake.

---

[3] Levette J. Davidson, "Mormon Songs," *Journal of American Folklore*, LVIII, No. 230 (October–December, 1945), 292.

[4] *Ibid.*, p. 252.

86. *Brigham, Brigham Young*

Old Brig-ham Young was a Mor-mon bold, And a lead-er
of the roar-ing rams, And a shep-herd of a heap of pret-ty
lit-tle sheep, And a nice fold of pret-ty lit-tle lambs.
And he lived with five and for-ty wives In the cit-y of
Great Salt Lake Where they woo and coo as pret-ty doves
do And cack-le like ducks to a drake. Brig-ham, Brig-ham
Young; 'Tis a mir-a-cle he sur-vives, With his roar-ing
rams, his pret-ty lit-tle lambs, And five and for-ty wives.

Chorus:
Brigham, Brigham Young;
    'Tis a miracle he survives,
With his roaring rams, his pretty little lambs,
    And five and forty wives.

Number forty-five was about sixteen,
    Number one was sixty-three,
And among such a riot how he ever keeps them quiet
    Is a right-down mystery to me.
For they clatter and they claw, and they jaw, jaw, jaw,
    Each one has a different desire;

It would aid the renown of the best shop in town
 To supply them with half what they require.

Old Brigham Young was a stout man once
 But now he is thin and old,
And I love to state, there's no hair on his pate
 Which once wore a covering of gold.
For his youngest wives won't have white wool
 And his old ones won't take red,
So in tearing it out they have taken turn about
 Till they've pulled all the wool from his head.

Now his boys sing songs all day,
 And his girls they all sing psalms;
And among such a crowd he has it pretty loud
 For they're as musical as Chinese Gongs.
And when they advance for a Mormon dance,
 He is filled with a greatest surprise,
For they're sure to end the night with a tabernacle fight
 And scratch out one another's eyes.

There never was a home like Brigham Young's,
 So curious and so queer,
For if his joys are double he has a terrible lot of trouble,
 For it gains on him year by year.
He sets in his state and bears his fate
 In a satisfied sort of way;
He has one wife to bury and one wife to marry
 And a new kid born every day.

Now if anybody envies Brigham Young,
 Let them go to Great Salt Lake,
And if they have leisure to examine at their pleasure
 They'll find it's a great mistake.
One wife at a time, so says my rhyme,
 Is enough for the proudest don,
So e'er you strive to live lord of forty-five
 Live happy if you can with one.

ᏩᎦ 87. *Zack, the Mormon Engineer* ᏩᎦ

This song is more comic than satiric in its picture of a Mormon Bishop, Zack Black, who was an engineer for the Denver and Rio Grande Railroad and had a wife in every town that he passed through. The contributor of the first version, L. M. Hilton, has sung the song for many collectors and for many audiences, and people think of it as being his song. He says that a Denver and Rio Grande Railroad publicity agent asked him for the song to use for promotion purposes. Rosalie Sorrels, Elayne Clark, and other folksingers sing it with delight. Mormon audiences have always liked it.

A

Sung by L. M. Hilton, Ogden, Utah, July 18, 1959.
Other sources: 70 Hilton; 71 Sorrels and Fife.

Old Zack he came to Utah
Way back in seventy-three,
A right good Mormon gentleman
And a Bishop too was he.
He drove a locomotive for the D. and R. G.,
With women he was popular,
As popular as could be,
And when he'd whistle—ooh! ooh!
Mamma'd understand
That Zack was headed homeward
On the Denver and Rio Grande.

Old Zack he had a wife-e
In every railroad town
No matter where he stopped
He had a place to lay him down,
And when his train was coming
He wanted her to know
So as he passed each wife-e's home
His whistle, he would blow,
And when he'd whistle—ooh! ooh!
Mamma'd understand
That Zack was headed homeward
On the Denver and Rio Grande.

87. *Zack, the Mormon Engineer*

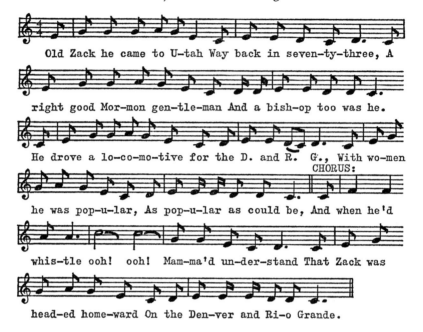

Old Zack he came to U-tah Way back in seven-ty-three, A right good Mor-mon gen-tle-man And a bish-op too was he. He drove a lo-co-mo-tive for the D. and R. G., With wo-men

CHORUS:

he was pop-u-lar, As pop-u-lar as could be, And when he'd whis-tle ooh! ooh! Mam-ma'd un-der-stand That Zack was head-ed home-ward On the Den-ver and Ri-o Grande.

Old Zack he claimed to love his wives
And love them all the same
But always his little Mabel
Was the one that he would name,
And as he would pass her
He'd blow his whistle loud,
And when she'd throw a kiss at him
Old Zack would look so proud,
And when he'd whistle—ooh! ooh!
Mamma'd understand
That Zack was headed homeward
On the Denver and Rio Grande.

Now listen everybody
Because this story's true
Old Zack he had a wife-e
In every town that he'd pass through.
They tried to make him transfer
Onto the old U. P.

But Zack said no, because his wives
Were on the D. and R. G.
And when he'd whistle—ooh! ooh!
Mamma'd understand
That Zack was headed homeward
On the Denver and Rio Grande.

B

Text from Levette Davidson, "Mormon Songs," Journal of American Folklore, *LVIII (October–December, 1945), 293. His source was Briegel,* Old Time Mormon and Far West Songs *(1933), pp. 38–39.*

Zack Black came to Utah back in Eighty-three,
A right good Mormon and a Bishop, too, was he,
He ran a locomotive on the "D'n'R. G.,"
And Zack was awful popular as you will see.

Chorus:
Hear him whistle!
He ran a locomotive on the "D'n'R. G."

Zack he had a wife in every town,
He numbered them from twelve 'way down to number two,
Oh, in his locomotive he'd go steaming 'round,
And when he'd pass each wifie's home his whistle blew.

Zack he always said he loved 'em all the same,
But wifie number twelve he loved her mighty well,
He had her picture mounted in his engine cab,
And when he passed her home he'd always ring the bell.

Listen ev'ry body, 'cause this story's true,
Zack had a wife in ev'ry town his train passed through.
They tried to shift Zack over to the old "U. P.,"
But Zack demurred, 'cause he preferred the "D'n'R. G."

88. *A Marriage Proposal*

The following "Mormon Love Serenade" could hardly be expected to win the hearts of fair ladies, but it no doubt brought laughs to listeners.

Text from Davidson, "Mormon Songs," Journal of American Folklore, *LVIII (October–December, 1945), 293.*
Other sources: 43 Hubbard 415.

Say, Susan, wilt thou come with me,
In sweet community to live
Oh heart and hand and home to thee,
A sixteenth part I'll freely give,
Of all the love that swells my breast,
Of all the honor of my name,
Of worldly wealth by me possessed,
A sixteenth portion thou shalt claim.

Nay, tell me not too many share
The blessings that I offer thee,
Thou'lt find but fifteen others there,
A household happy, gay and free.
A mod'rate household, I may say,
My neighbor has as many more
And Brother Brigham, o'er the way,
Luxuriates in forty-four.

I'll give thee whatso'er thou wilt,
So it but be a sixteenth part,
'Twould be the deepest depth of guilt,
To slight the rest who share my heart.
Then wilt thou not thy fraction yield,
To make complete my perfect bliss?
Say "yes" and let our joy be sealed,
With just the sixteenth of a kiss.

♋ 89. *The Mormon Coon* ♋

Typical of hyperbolic satire which appeared in vaudeville is this number which sounds as if it had been influenced by Negro minstrels.

Text from Davidson, "Mormon Songs," Journal of American Folklore, LVIII (October–December, 195), 292 (Virgil V. Peterson, Denver, Colorado, who learned it from a Mormon missionary). Other source: 43 Hubbard 420.

Young Abraham left home one day;
Nobody knew just why he went away
Until a friend of his received a note.
It was from Abe and this is what he wrote:

I'm out in Utah in the Mormon land
I'm not coming home, 'cause I'm a living grand
I used to rave about a single life
Now every day I get a brand new wife.

Chorus:
I got a big brunette
I got a blonde petite
I got 'em short, fat, thin, and tall
I got a Zulu pal
I got a Cuban gal
They come in bunches when I call
Now—that ain't all.
I got a homely few
I got 'em pretty too
I got 'em black as the octoroon
I can cut a figure eight
I must ship them by freight
For I am a Mormon Coon.

There's one girl that ain't married yet, they say;
I'm saving her up for a rainy day.
If for every girl I had a single cent,
Then the picture gallery I could rent.
I got me many of a homely lot;
I keep the marriage license door bell hot.

If a wife upon the street I chance to run,
I have to ask her, "What's your number, Hon?"

∽ 90. *Sweet Betsy from Pike* ∽

Nearly every song collection of the western states has a version of "Sweet Betsy from Pike." The stanza referring to Brigham Young in this variant is typical of folk emendation and additions. Mormons sang versions without the Brigham Young reference as well as with it. Hubbard's version has no Utah reference; Fife's has the following lines:

> She rode down the mountain with her lover Ike
> When Brigham saw Betsy he asked her to stay
> When Betsy said, no, Brigham brayed like a mule.

A version I collected from Jay Healy, Provo, Utah, in 1959 has the following stanza:

> They came down the mountain into old Salt Lake
> Where Betsy met Brigham one evening quite late;
> He asked her to stay, but Betsy said, "No";
> Brigham said, "If you don't, to Hell you will go."

Sung by Ray Decker, Provo, Utah, November, 1959.
  Other sources: 43 Hubbard 300–301, 68 Fife MC I, 618 (Buck Lee, Clearfield, Utah, 1946).

Oh, don't you remember sweet Betsy from Pike
Who crossed the mountains with her lover Ike
With two yoke of oxen, a large yellow dog,
A tall Shanghai rooster, and one spotted hog.

One evening quite early they camped on the Platte
Close by the roadside on a green shady flat
When Betsy, sure footed, lay down to repose
With wonder she gazed on his Pike County nose.

The Shanghai ran off and the cattle all died;
The last piece of bacon that morning was fried.
Poor Ike was discouraged and Betsy was mad;
The dog wagged his tail and looked wonderfully sad.

At length the old wagon came down with a crash
And out on the prairie rolled all kinds of trash,
A few little baby clothes, done up with great care,
Looked rather suspicious though all on the square.

They went by Salt Lake to inquire the way
Where Brigham declared Sweet Betsy should stay.
Betsy got frightened and ran like a deer
While Brigham stood pawing the ground like a steer.

91. *The Good Old Yankee Doodle*

The spirit of bacchanalian mirth which pervades the last song continues in the tone of this one. "The Mormons are a jolly set" who "believe in serving God as they have a mind to." And their merriment is carried so far as to include marrying more than one wife. The apparent import of the song is to point out the irony of these people choosing to call the practice of plural marriage a serving of God. Non-Mormons singing about the Mormons see the merriment variously from mild to violent sacrilege. Mormons themselves, however, are proud of their ability to be "jolly" and often quote their scriptural adage "Man is that he might have joy." This ratiocination is evident in various areas throughout this book.

Text from Austin and Alta Fife, Saints of Sage and Saddle, *p. 331.*
Other sources: 68 Fife MC III, 127 (Fife says, "Text is from George W. Johnson, Jottings by the Way, A Collection of Rustic Rhyme . . . . *St. George, Utah. Printed by C. E. Johnson, 1882, pp. 22–23)"; 71 Sorrels and Fife.*

Yankee Doodle is the tune some Yankee chap invented,
To sing on Independence Day to make us feel contented;
Now Independence Day has come, as many have before us,
We'll sing again the good old tune and all join in the chorus.

Chorus:
Yankee Doodle is the tune the Mormons find so handy
To sing on Independence Day, old Yankee Doodle Dandy.

The Mormons are a jolly set, they come from every nation,
From every country, every clime, in all this broad creation;
They all believe in serving God just as they have a mind to,
And marry one wife, two, or three, just as they feel inclined to.

They all believe that Washington the founder of the nation,
Was called of God to do that work and led by inspiration;
They think the laws our Fathers made, were what they were
    intended;
They've stood the test a hundred years and need not be amended.

There are some fellows now so smart they've got in their noodle,
That Mormon Boys can take the lead in playing Yankee Doodle;
So they are trying very hard to make a clear solution,
By tearing up old Seventy-six and change the Constitution.

☙ 92. *Don't Marry the Mormon Boys* ☙

The composer of this song wrote it as a parody to "Texas Boys."
The Fifes have observed that "Texas Boys" is itself a parody of a
song sung all along the frontier, that some texts are long and sug-
gestive and some "even openly scandalous." It appears to be a
woman's advice to young girls not to marry the Mormon boys, for
to do so means to give up joy, eat johnny cake, go to meetings, and
bear children. This version differs from other versions referred to
below in that it gives emphasis to the burden of childbearing in
each verse. Mormon philosophy has disapproved birth control and
advocated acceptance in marriage of all the children Heaven sends.

*Text from Eliza Jane Avery, Burley, Idaho, August, 1932. Music
from 71 Fife and Sorrels.*

*Other sources: 43 Hubbard 424; 68 Fife MC I, 525 (Paul Ander-
son, Bountiful, Utah, 1946); 71 Sorrels and Fife.*

Come, girls, come and listen to my noise.
Don't you marry the Mormon boys,
For if you do your fortune it will be
Johnny cake and babies is all you'll see.

92. *Don't Marry the Mormon Boys*

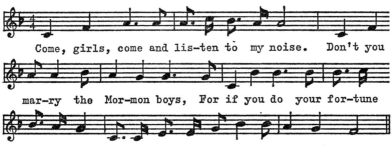

Come, girls, come and lis-ten to my noise. Don't you

mar-ry the Mor-mon boys, For if you do your for-tune

it will be John-ny cake and bab-ies is all you'll see.

Chorus:
Milk your cow and milk her in a pail;
Take it to the kitchen, hang it on a nail.

If you don't want to work and give up your joys,
Don't you marry the Mormon boys;
They'll load you with babies and send you to meeting
And make you work for all you're getting.

93. *The Merry Mormons*

The new frontier religion approved drama, singing, and "round" dancing. The last line of this song makes plain the composer's purpose to satirize the Mormons in pointing out the egoistic image they have of themselves. The solidarity of the people as reflected in such things as marrying "none but Mormons" and thinking of themselves as chosen people and others as "Gentiles" could hardly please the nonmember. What the Mormon exults over in ecstatic joy, the non-Mormon speaks of in mild derision: "I never knew what joy was/'Til I became a Mormon."

Text from Davidson, "Mormon Songs," Journal of American Folklore, *LVIII (October–December, 1945), 282.*[5]

[5] Davidson says, "Sent to me by John D. Spenser of Salt Lake. According to A. B. Carlton, *The Wonderland of the Wild West* (n.p., 1891), this son [sic] was popular in the rural districts of Mormon land in the 'eighties. He included one stanza and the chorus in his book."

Tune: "The Bonnie Breast Knots."

What peace and joy pervade my soul—
What sweet sensations o'er me roll;
And love predominates the whole,
   Since I became a Mormon.

Chorus:
Hey, the merry, ho the merry,
   Hey the merry Mormons;
I never knew what joy was
   'Til I became a Mormon.

At night the Mormons they convene,
To chat a while, or sing a hymn,
Or perchance repeat a rhyme
   They've made about the Mormons.

To Sabbath meetings they repair—
Both old and young assemble there,
The words of inspired men to share—
   No less will suit the Mormons.

As ancient Israel's youths denied
To wed with those whom Heaven defied,
So modern Israel's youths have cried—
   We'll marry none but Mormons.

The Mormon father likes to see
His Mormon fam'ly all agree—
The prattling infant on his knee
   Cries, Papa, I'm a Mormon!

O, be our home,—the Mormons cry,—
Our place of birth, and where we die—
Celestialized and purified—
   The earth for perfect Mormons.

ᏏᎥᎧ 94. *Christine LeRoy* ᏏᎥᎧ

Little has been written about the heartache which may have
come to the first wife of a Mormon man when he brought home a
new wife, a beautiful young girl, to introduce to his old faithful
companion. Rosalie Sorrels of Salt Lake City sings this song and
relates it to Utah polygamy and a sorrow which accompanied plural
marriage. The song treats the universal problem of jealousy and
suffering because of unrequited love. The adaptation of an old story
to a new situation often occurs in folksong, thus giving more than
one factual basis for the action. Adaptation of this song to a polygamous situation is a natural thing; the old wife could well be jealous
of the dark-eyed Christine LeRoy who won the heart of her husband.
The wife in this song, who grieves bitterly but does not act, is unlike
the wronged woman in "Frankie and Johnny" ballads. She is more
nearly representative of submissive plural wives in the Mormon
society than is the revengeful Frankie type.

Sung by Jenny Hancock, Provo, Utah, August 25, 1959.

No, brother, 'twill never be better,
 'Tis useless to tell me so now,
My broken heart only is waiting
 For a resting place under the snow.
I only was dreaming, dear brother,
 How happy our home was with joy
When a serpent crept into our Eden
 In the fair form of Christine LeRoy.

I was dreaming again of our bridal,
 One year ago only tonight;
As I blushed 'neath the gaslights above me
 In my jewels and garments so white,
When she came with the face of an angel
 And wished us our lifetime of joy;
My heart sank within at the meeting
 Of those dark eyes of Christine LeRoy.

When she gave her soft hand to my husband,
 I knew that he thought me a toy
Beside this fair radiant glory,
 This beautiful Christine LeRoy.

94. *Christine LeRoy*

No, broth-er, 'twill nev-er be bet-ter, 'Tis use-less to tell me so now, My brok-en heart on-ly is wait-ing For a rest-ing place un-der the snow.

Her diamonds shone bright in her tresses
   Falling back from her fair waxen brow
And sparkled like stars in the gaslights
   On her fingers as white as the snow.

So time wore away, and my husband
   Grew thoughtless and careworn each day,
And I know 'twas the wiles of a demon
   That had artfully lured him astray.
'Til at last one bright evening I found them,
   A sight all my life to destroy,
Hand in hand with her head on his shoulder
   Sat my Harry and Christine LeRoy.

So brother, be kind to your darling;
   Her poor heart is stricken and faint
At the thought of the wiles of a demon
   'Neath the beautiful face of a saint;
When I sleep under snowdrifts in winter
   Where no grief or no pain can destroy,
You can tell them they murdered me, brother;
   God forgive him and Christine LeRoy.

🌀 95. *Porter Rockwell* 🌀

No more colorful character has been a part of the Mormon culture than Orin Porter Rockwell, or "Old Port" as he was familiarly called. He is spoken of as the Danite, Brigham Young's Destroying Angel, and the Terror of the Plains. A friend, patron, and rugged protector of Joseph Smith, he became a loyal follower of Brigham Young. To cope with horse thieves and lawless men in pioneer Deseret, fearless men were needed to enforce order. Porter Rockwell has been described as one who was friendly disposed, jovial, and a devil-may-care type who was never outwitted by lawless men.

Traditionally Rockwell wore a long beard. As legend goes, the Prophet Joseph Smith told him his life would be preserved from violent death if he never cut his hair. This it appears provided him with a sense of invulnerability and a cool trigger hand. He is quoted as having said, "I never killed anybody who didn't deserve it." However, it appears that a good many deserved it, for as a law officer he always brought his man in, dead or alive.

This poem, "Porter Rockwell," originated among some Utah "Gentiles." Later it was set to music to the tune of "Solomon Levi," and it is still sung by many people both in and outside of the Church.

From Nicholas Van Alfen, Porter Rockwell, The Mormon Frontier Marshall, *p. 157.*

> Have you heard of Porter Rockwell?
> He's the Mormon triggerite.
> They say he hunts for horse thieves
> When the moon is shining bright.
> So if you rustle cattle,
> I'll tell you what to do,
> Get the drop on Porter Rockwell
> Or he'll get the drop on you.
>
> They say that Porter Rockwell
> Is a scout for Brigham Young—
> He's hunting up the unsuspects
> That haven't yet been hung.
> So if you steal a Mormon girl
> I'll tell you what to do,
> Get the drop on Porter Rockwell
> Or he'll get the drop on you.

ᏭᎤ 96. *Wheat* ᏭᎤ

Orin Porter Rockwell used the word "wheat" to mean good. The folk tell of his insisting that others join him in a "square drink," which meant unadulterated whiskey. Porter would raise the drink to his lips and with a twinkle in his eye say, "wheat" and drain the container to the bottom. Olive Burt says his war cry was "Wheat!" signifying that the wheat would be saved but the tares would be taken. She reports as follows: "My mother's scrapbook contains verses, rather better than most, which show how some folks felt about the long-haired character."

Text from Olive Woolley Burt (from her mother's scrapbook), American Murder Ballads, *p. 115.*

Old Port Rockwell has work to do,
So he saddles his sorrel and rides away;
And those who are watching wonder who
Will be a widow at break of day.
The waiting wife in the candle light,
Starts up as she hears a wild hoof-beat,
Then shrinks in terror as down the night
Comes the wailing of Port's dread war cry, "Wheat!"

Wheat!
She looks at her babes and tries to pray,
For she knows she's a widow and orphans are they.
Old Port Rockwell looks like a man,
With a beard on his face and his hair in a braid,
But there's none in the West but Brigham who can
Look in his eyes and not be afraid.
For Port is a devil in human shape,
Though he calls himself "Angel," says vengeance is sweet;
But he's black, bitter death, and there's no escape
When he wails through the night his dread war cry, "Wheat!"

Wheat!
Somewhere a wife with her babes kneels to pray,
For she knows she's a widow and orphans are they.

༄ 97. *The Kanab Tragedy* ༄

In this dry, western land blood has often been spilt for water, because water is the life blood of the people. This murder ballad from Olive Burt's collection deals with a murder over stolen water. Of it Mrs. Burt says:

The only feuding ballad I have from Utah recounts a locally famous case. It happened on a hot Sunday morning, July 23, 1899, in Kanab, a small settlement in the southwestern part of the state. It seems that the reservoir had been constructed on land belonging to Dan Seegmiller, and for various reasons his next neighbor, William Roundy, had long felt that Seegmiller was depriving him of his fair share of water. So bitter had the controversy become that both families looked with hatred at each other.

On this Sunday morning, Roundy told his son to take the water, as it was their turn. But when the young man went to the headgate, he found the canal dry. He came back and reported to his father. Roundy leaped upon his horse and, shotgun in hand, rode to the reservoir. It, too, was empty. Incensed, Roundy rode to Seegmiller's yard, tethered his horse at the corral, strode up to the cabin door, and knocked loudly. Mrs. Seegmiller answered and turned to call her husband. By the time Seegmiller appeared at the door, Roundy was walking toward the corral. Seegmiller followed. There was an angry exchange. Suddenly Roundy raised his gun and shot Seegmiller, who fell to the ground, writhing. A man named Snyder, who worked for Seegmiller, saw his employer fall and yelled at Roundy. Roundy shouted back, "If you want me, Mr. Snyder, you will find me at my house." He then pumped two more shots into Seegmiller, who had staggered to his feet and was running for shelter.

Roundy leaped upon his horse and started for home. As he passed his brother's place he called out, "Tell Father that I've killed Seegmiller!" Arriving at his house, he went inside, told his wife and son what he had done, shook hands solemnly with them, and turned toward the door. His wife tried to stop him, but he said, "I must go. Snyder is after me with a gun." Roundy had no sooner got out of sight than a shot was heard. Rushing out, his wife and son found Roundy dying on the ground. He had taken his own life. [6]

Text from Burt (from her mother's papers), American Murder Ballads, *pp. 243–244.*

> In Kanab they will always remember
> This Twenty-Fourth of July

[6] Olive W. Burt, *American Murder Ballads,* pp. 241–242.

For this year there's no celebration,
No band plays and no pennants fly.

The speeches they give in the Church house,
Do not boast of our brave Pioneers;
There's no shouting, no dancing, no picnic,
But there's sorrow and mourning and tears.

For two of the town's best men are lying
In their coffins awaiting the earth;
[Line illegible where paper was folded]
There's no room in our hearts now for mirth.

It happened because of hot anger—
A quarrel about their water right,
William Roundy accused Dan Seegmiller
Of stealing his turn in the night.

So Roundy jumped up on his pony,
Rode right down to Seegmiller's door;
He shouted, "Come out and I'll show you,
You'll not steal my turn any more!"

And Dan, little thinking of trouble,
Came out with his babe in his arm;
His wife Emma stood there beside him,
Neither yet felt the faintest alarm.

Then Roundy quick lifted his shotgun—
Aimed it straight at Dan Seegmiller's heart;
Emma screamed and ran forward to stop him,
[Another illegible line]

Dan fell to the ground with his boy,
Weeping, poor Emma knelt down,
Not knowing if both husband and baby
Were dead beside her on the ground.

Roundy turned then and rode to his own house,
Where he kissed his wife fondly goodbye,
Then out into the yard he staggered,
By his own cruel hand there to die.

So today there is no celebration,
Kanab has no thought for Pioneers;
Two fine men now lie in their coffins—
No wonder the town's bathed in tears!

98. *The Orderville Murder*[7]

In small towns a tragic murder such as that told in this ballad is
not an everyday occurrence. In fact, its pathetic horror often becomes the topic of conversation and song for years. However, the
shocking story told here is not uncommon in the world; many
murders have been committed with the same motivation.

Mormons established a community farm, a United Order, as it
was called, and named the center Orderville. The experiment in
communal living succeeded there for a time. It was at this south-
central Utah settlement that the murder and confession occurred
and from which this ballad emerged.

Text from the collection of Olive W. Burt, Salt Lake City.

Mary Steavens she had disappeared
And nobody knew where.
Her mother was so worried,
Her face was lined with care.
The neighbors said, "We'll go and look
Up Gordon Hollow way."
For Mary was seen walking there
Upon that April day.

They went to Gordon Hollow
And there the searchers found
A pool of blood that had seeped up
From underneath the ground.
It had been covered over
With a layer of red sand,
But it had seeped up through this
Like an avenging hand.

[7] This is the town referred to in Song No. 35, "The United Order."

They looked about more carefully
And where some boulders sat
They saw the bright blue ribbon
Of Mary Steaven's hat.
They pulled away the boulders,
And underneath the stack
They found poor Mary's body
With four bullets in the back.

Now all the town was worried.
Who could have done this deed?
They looked about for other clues
And found one they could read.
It was some deep-made footprints
That made a wandering track—
Two sets to Gordon Hollow,
But just one coming back.

They got the shoes of every man
That lived in Orderville
To see if any fit those tracks—
Alvin Heaton's filled the bill.
The folks would not believe it;
Alvin was a favorite.
They shook their heads and muttered—
That clue was not read right.

But Alvin was arrested
Placed in Kane County jail;
He listened to the charges;
His courage did not fail.
Justice Ford he kept a-questioning,
The whole county was distressed.
Then when no one was expecting it,
Alvin Heaton he confessed.

He said he'd been friends with Mary,
And had promised to be true;
She wanted him to marry her,
For a wedding was her due.
He begged her not to press him,
Some excuses must be found;

For she was not attractive—
She weighed two hundred pounds.

Mary said the law would force him
To give their child his name;
And when he couldn't change her mind
He played his well-planned game.
He'd brought a shotgun with him,
And he walked slow in the track,
And when he was well behind her
He shot her in the back.

He dragged her to the stream bed,
And covered her with rocks.
Then he saw blood upon the ground;
It gave him quite a shock.
He tried to cover it with sand
And then he hurried home
And began to clean the stable
So none would know that he had roamed.

Now there was no gainsaying
This confession—it rang true.
So Alvin was convicted,
It was all the court could do.
And now he lies in prison,
As many a youth has done,
Who tried to avoid his duty
By the use of a shotgun.

৩৯৯ 99. *The Double Tragedy* ৩৯৯

Of this ballad Mrs. Burt says:

Another Utah Pioneer Day was marked with tragedy which inspired a ballad. It was July 24, 1891, and Monticello, a small community on the east slope of the Abajo Mountains in southeastern Utah, was holding its third Pioneer Day celebration. The town had been founded late in 1887, when the Mormon Church had "called" five families to settle the site. As with most early Utah celebrations, the affair took the form of a dance, with supper to be served later in the evening. Everyone came, not only the settlers, but scattered ranchers of the area, cowboys and sheepherders, and Indians.

The dance was at its height, with the fiddler fiddling and the dancers hoeing it down, when Tom Roach, very drunk, came out onto the floor, flourishing his gun and sending the merrymakers scurrying to the wall. Joe McCord, a friend of Roach's, stepped forward and tried to persuade the fellow to desist from his foolishness, for that is what McCord considered it. But Roach was too far gone to listen to reason and shot his friend dead, there in front of the crowd.

Mrs. Jane Walton, one of the original settlers and a woman of influence in the community, stepped toward Roach and began to plead with him to throw down his gun. The killer seemed to listen, and the revelers breathed a little more freely. But Frank Adams had slipped out of the hall and gone for a gun. Now he returned and entered the room. Seeing Roach standing close to Mrs. Walton, and fearing for her life, Adams shot. At that moment the killer moved and the bullet struck the woman, killing her.

Roach slipped away now, found a horse and made for the mountains. He hid in the rocks near Verdure, six miles south of Monticello. A posse went after him, but as they drew close Roach yelled for them to stop. He had the drop on them, and a further attempt to capture him meant certain death. The officers turned back. They rounded up more help and went to surround Roach, but he had escaped into Arizona and never was apprehended.

Albert R. Lyman, long-time resident of the southeastern corner of Utah, from whom I obtained the details of the affair, commented, "It is a long story, with many angles." The ballad concerning the "Double Tragedy" was given to me by Dr. Austin Fife, who obtained it from Otho Murphy, of Moab, the author and composer.

Text from Burt, American Murder Ballads, *p. 245.*

Other source: 68 Fife MC I, 606 (Otho Murphy, Moab, Utah, 1946).

Tune: "The Blind Child."

> Bright lights were shining in the hall,
> Everyone seemed happy and gay;
> Making merry one and all
> As by music they did sway.
> Tripping feet of dainty maid,
> Scuffing feet of booted men,
> Laughing remarks to pardners made,
> Rang out o'er mountain glen.
>
> When quickly out upon the floor
> In anger strode Tom Roach,

His gun was glistening in his hand,
There was no one to reproach.
At the bark of gun the startled crowd
Whirled 'round toward the door.
The smoke was billowing as a shroud
About the gunman on the floor.

"Out, file out, everybody out,
Speed up all," cried he.
He knew not what he was about,
He was filled with raw whiskey.
Men and women in grasping dread,
Fled out upon the street,
When with a shout and flying lead,
He cut off their retreat.

Now there are some that may return,
But others out must stay;
With planted feet and countenance stern
He forced them to obey.
Then walked up in confidence,
Smiling, came McCord.
He said to Tom, "You'll let me in,
For I've always been your pard."

But with a flick of gun Tom barred his way.
"Not another step," he said.
McCord advanced that fatal step
And Roach's gun belched lead.
A look of surprise flashed in his eyes,
"Roach, you've killed me," he said.
And with a last heartbreaking sigh,
At Roach's feet fell dead.

The music swelled in sweet refrain,
The floorman gave his call;
"Swing your pardners to the set!
Let's on, boys, with the ball."
Mrs. Walton standing by,
With gentle voice did plead,
And Tom with ever calming eye
Her quieting voice did heed.

When suddenly within the door
Frank Adams sprang.
In his hand a Winchester bore.
His voice loudly rang.
"Roach!" Roach swayed aside,
As the trigger was pressed,
And Mrs. Walton falling died
With a bullet in her breast.

The confusion of the moment
Of this last tragedy
Was the cover by which Roach
In silent haste did flee;
The fatal shot that Adams fired,
When in anger driven,
By Mrs. Walton's friends and kin
Was in deep sorrow forgiven.

100. *Mountain Meadows Massacre*

In the spring of 1857, a band of one hundred and thirty-six emigrants from Missouri and Arkansas set out for southern California. The party had about six hundred head of cattle, thirty wagons, and thirty horses and mules.

Because of the coming of Johnston's Army to Utah and the imminent threat of war between the United States and the Mormons, the Saints had been ordered not to furnish any emigrant trains with supplies. This order made it difficult for the Arkansas and Missouri emigrants to get provisions after reaching the Mormon country.

Antagonisms developed between them and the Mormons. Part of the trouble may have been engendered through the revengeful spirit the Mormons held because many, especially the older folk, still vividly remembered the persecutions they had received from Missourians.

The party, having passed through Cedar City where they had succeeded in getting some wheat, had camped at an isolated spot northwest of St. George in Washington County, Utah.

Of the massacre, Olive Burt says:

Just before daybreak on Monday or Tuesday, September 7 or 8, the emigrant train was attacked by a large band of Paiutes and white men. The emigrants fought off the attack and, entrenched behind their wagons, remained there till Friday morning, when the attackers sent William Bateman with a flag of truce to the beseiged. They parleyed, and it was agreed that all arms and ammunition of the emigrants should be placed in a wagon. The wounded members of the band were to be put in another wagon, and the Mormon "rescuers" would then conduct the Arkansans safely to Cedar City. The emigrants, actually having no choice, accepted the offer in good faith.

About noon, John D. Lee, one of the white men in the attacking party and a prominent Mormon, led the Arkansans into the open, where a double file of settlers of southern Utah was drawn up. As the unarmed emigrants passed slowly along in single file, Indians and whites opened fire, killing the entire company with the exception of a few children who were considered "too young to talk."

All the participants were sworn to secrecy, but such a terrible deed could not be hidden, and before long the shocked country was demanding redress. After "Johnston's Army" arrived in 1858, an investigation was made and the guilt of several of the Saints in southern Utah was established. These men kept out of reach of the law, however, until 1874, when John D. Lee was arrested and tried at Beaver, Utah. At his first trial, the jury disagreed, but in 1876 he was tried again and convicted. On March 23, 1877, nearly twenty years after the crime, Lee was taken to the Mountain Meadows and shot. He was the only person punished for the crime committed by many, and calmer judgment now absolves him of some of the responsibility for the tragedy. All evidence indicates that these southern Utah men were acting on their own initiative, and that Brigham Young and other Church authorities three hundred miles away in Salt Lake City had no knowledge of the affair until it was an accomplished fact.

The marker at the Mountain Meadows bears a bronze plaque on which is inscribed:

MOUNTAIN MEADOWS
A FAVORITE RECRUITING PLACE ON
THE OLD SPANISH TRAIL

In this vicinity—September 7–11, 1857, occured one of the most lamentable tragedies in the history annals of the west. A company of about 140 emigrants from Arkansas and Missouri led by Captain Charles Fancher, en route to California, was attacked by white men and Indians. All but 17 small children were killed. John D. Lee, who confessed to participation as leader, was legally executed here March 23rd, 1877. Most of the emigrants were buried in their own defense pit. This monument was reverently dedicated September 10th, 1932, by the Utah Pioneer Trails and Landmarks Association and the people of Southern Utah.

The horror of this massacre is shocking to Mormons and non-Mormons alike. Historians and folklorists find the subject fascinating to study. The truths and untruths of the events are so mixed that one finds it difficult to know the facts. The most scholarly work on the subject is Juanita Brooks' *Mountain Meadows Massacre*.

For a more thorough study of this particular ballad, the student should see Fife's article in *Western Folklore*[8] in which he presents three basic versions. One of these is a photographic copy of a column from the *Ely White Pine News*, Ely, Nevada, March 19, 1870, p. 3.[9] It is a short version of the song and, although it gives the basic story, it is the least complete of the Fife versions. It is presented here for comparison:

> In Indian garb and color
> Those bloody hounds were seen,
> To flock around that little train,
> All on the meadow green.
>
> To see mothers and their children
> All flowing in their gore,
> Oh such an awful sight, I think
> Was never seen before!
>
> Then Lee, the leader of this band,
> To them, his word did give,
> That if their arms they would give up
> He'd surely let them live.
>
> But when their arms they did give up,
> And turned for Cedar City,
> They rushed on them in Indian style,
> Oh, what a human pity!
>
> They melted down with one accord,
> Like wax before the flame;
> Both men and women, old and young;
> Oh, Utah! blush for shame!
>
> By order of their General
> This deed was done, you see;
> The leader of this wicked band,
> His name was John D. Lee.
>
> Then afterward they tried to clean
> Themselves of all the shame,
> And to get out the best they could;
> The Indians bear the blame.

---

[8] Austin E. Fife, "Mountain Meadows Massacre," *Western Folklore*, XII, No. 4 (October, 1953), 229–237.

[9] *Ibid.*, p. 237 (reprinted from *Ely White Pine News*, October, 1933).

People are not prone to publicize derogatory matter about themselves; a song about this horrible affair is naturally taboo among the Mormons. As a song collector, I have found several older people who have let me see the song as they have copied it, but all refused to give it to me for my collection. Of the version printed here, Olive Burt says: "All the versions are incomplete in places, but as all are obviously the same ballad, I have supplied missing stanzas of one version from the other two to produce a complete ballad of the 'Mountain Meadows Massacre.'"

Text from Burt, American Murder Ballads, *p. 118.*

Other sources: 41 Fife 229–241; 43 Hubbard 445; 65 Toelken 169–172; 68 Fife MC I, 818 (J. F. Chesley, Reseda, California, 1951); five other entries in the Fife Collection.

100. *Mountain Meadows Massacre*

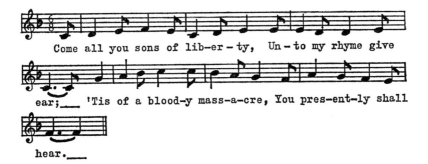

Come all you sons of liberty,
Unto my rhyme give ear;
'Tis of a bloody massacre,
You presently shall hear.

In splendor on the mountains
Some thirty wagons came,
They were awaited by a wicked band,
Oh, Utah! Where's thy shame?

On a crisp October morning
At the Mountain Meadows green,
By the light of bright campfires,
Lee's Mormon bullets screamed.

In Indian garb and colors
Those bloody hounds were seen
To attack the little train
All on the meadows green.

They were attacked in the morning,
As they were on their way,
They forthwith coralled their wagons,
And fought in blood array.

When Lee, the leader of the band,
His word to them did give,
That if their arms they would give up
He'd surely let them live.

When once their arms they had give up,
Thinking their lives to save,
The words were broken among the rest,
Which sent them to their grave.

When once they had give up their arms
And started for Cedar City,
They rushed on them in Indian style,
Oh, what a human pity!

They melted down with one accord,
Like wax before the flame;
Both men and women, young and old,
Oh, Utah! Where's thy shame?

Both men and women, young and old,
A-rolling in their gore,
And such an awful sight and scene
Was ne'er beheld before!

Their property was divided,
Among this bloody crew;
And Uncle Sam is bound to see
This bloody matter through.

The soldiers will be stationed
Throughout this Utah land,
All for to find those murderers out
And bring them to his hand.

By order of their president
This awful deed was done,
He was the leader of the Mormon Church,
His name was Brigham Young.

BIBLIOGRAPHY

Published Works on Mormon History

1. Alfen, Nicholas Van. *Porter Rockwell, the Mormon Frontier Marshal.* Logan, Utah: L.D.S. Institute of Religion, 1964.
2. Bancroft, Hubert Howe. *History of Utah.* San Francisco: The History Co., 1891.
3. Berrett, William Edwin. *Doctrines of the Restored Church.* Salt Lake City: Deseret Book Company, 1941.
4. ———, and Alma P. Burton. *Readings in L.D.S. Church History.* Salt Lake City: Deseret Book Company, 1953.
5. *Book of Mormon.* Salt Lake City: Church of Jesus Christ of Latter-day Saints, 1923.
6. Brodie, Fawn M. *No Man Knows My History: The Life of Joseph Smith.* New York: Knopf, 1945.
7. Brooks, Juanita (ed.). "Journal of Thales Haskell," *Utah Historical Quarterly,* V, No. 12, (January–April 1944), 1–2.
8. ———. *The Mountain Meadows Massacre.* Stanford, California: Stanford University Press, 1950.
9. Carter, Kate. *Heart Throbs.* Vol. 10. Salt Lake City: Daughters of the Utah Pioneers, 1959.
10. Evans, John Henry. *One Hundred Years of Mormonism.* Salt Lake City: Deseret News Press, 1905.
11. Golder, Grant A. *March of the Mormon Battalion.* New York: The Century Company, 1928.
12. Hafen, LeRoy R., and Ann W. Hafen. *Handcarts to Zion.* The Far West and The Rockies Series, Vol. 14. Glendale, California: A. H. Clark Co., 1960.
13. Larson, Andrew Karl. *The Red Hills of November.* Salt Lake City: Deseret News Press, 1957.
14. Mack, Lucy. *Biographical Sketches of Joseph Smith and His Progenitors.* Liverpool: Church of Jesus Christ of Latter-day Saints, 1853.
15. O'dea, Thomas F. *The Mormons.* Chicago: University of Chicago Press, 1957.
16. Richards, Franklin D., and S. W. Richards. *Brigham Young's Discourses.* 26 vols. Liverpool: Church of Jesus Christ of Latter-day Saints, 1854–1886. Reprint edition, Los Angeles: Gartner Printing and Litho Co., Inc., 1956.
17. Roberts, Brigham H. *A Comprehensive History of the Church of Jesus Christ of Latter-day Saints.* 6 vols. Salt Lake City: Deseret News Press, 1930.
18. Smith, Joseph, Jr. *History of the Church of Jesus Christ of Latter-day Saints.* 6 vols. Salt Lake City: Deseret Book Co., 1904.

19. ———. *The Doctrine and Covenants of the Church of Jesus Christ of Latter-day Saints*. Salt Lake City: Church of Jesus Christ of Latter-day Saints, 1923.

20. Spencer, Clarissa Young, and Mable Harmon. *One Who Was Valiant*. Caldwell, Idaho: Caxton Printers, 1940.

21. Stegner, Wallace. *Mormon Country*. New York: Duell, Sloan and Pearce, 1942.

22. Stenhouse, Thomas B. H. *The Rocky Mountain Saints*. New York: D. Appleton and Co., 1873.

23. Tyler, Daniel. *A Concise History of the Mormon Battalion in the Mexican War*. Salt Lake City, 1881. Photographic reprint by Rio Grande Press, Inc., Chicago, 1964.

24. West, Ray B., Jr. *Kingdom of the Saints*. New York: The Viking Press, 1957.

25. Widtsoe, John A. (ed.). *Brigham Young's Discourses*. Salt Lake City: Deseret Book Company, 1925.

Unpublished Theses on Folksong of the Mormons

26. Cheney, Thomas E. "Folk Ballad Characteristics in a Modern Collection of Songs." University of Idaho, Moscow, 1936.

27. Lauridsen, Cora Burt. "An Analytical and Comparative Study of Folk Music of Modern Inspiration." Occidental College, Los Angeles, 1948.

28. Shumway, Lenn M. "A Collection of Ballads . . . from Taylor Arizona." Brigham Young University, Provo, Utah, 1957.

29. Terry, Elvis B. "A Collection of Ballads and Folk Songs from Enterprise, Utah." Brigham Young University, Provo, Utah, 1951.

Published Works on Folksong of the Mormons

30. Botkin, Benjamin A. *A Treasury of Western Folklore*. New York: Crown Publishers, 1951.

31. Burt, Olive Woolley. *Murder Ballads and Their Stories*. New York: Oxford University Press, 1958.

32. ———. "Murder Ballads of Mormondom," *Western Folklore*, XVIII, No. 2 (April 1959), 121–130.

33. Cheney, Thomas E. "Bringing the Desert into Blossom," *Utah Music Educator*, VIII, No. 3 (Fall 1963), 9–15.

34. Child, Francis James. *English and Scottish Popular Ballads*. 5 vols. New York: The Folklore Press, 1956.

35. Davidson, Levette J. "Mormon Songs," *Journal of American Folklore*, LVIII, No. 230 (October–December 1945), 273–300.

36. Davis, John (Ieuan, pseudonym). *The Bee Hive Songster*. Salt Lake City: Daily Telegraph Office, 1868.

37. Dorson, Richard M. *American Folklore*. Chicago: University of Chicago Press, 1959.

38. ———. *Buying the Wind*. Chicago: University of Chicago Press, 1964.

39. Durham, Alfred. *Pioneer Songs*. Salt Lake City: Daughters of Utah Pioneers, 1932.

40. Fife, Austin E. "Folksongs of Mormon Inspiration," *Western Folklore*, VI, No. 1 (January 1947), 42–52.

41. ———. "Mountain Meadows Massacre," *Western Folklore*, XII, No. 4 (October 1953), 229–241.

42. ———, and Alta Fife. *Saints of Sage and Saddle*. Bloomington: Indiana University Press, 1956.

43. Hubbard, Lester A. *Ballads and Songs from Utah*. Salt Lake City: University of Utah Press, 1961.

44. ———. "Militant Songs of the Mormons," *Western Folklore*, XVIII, No. 2 (April 1959), 121–130.

45. ———. "Songs and Ballads of the Utah Pioneers," *Utah Humanities Review*, I, No. 1 (January 1947), 74–96.

46. Ives, Burl. *The Burl Ives Song Book*. New York: Ballantine Books, 1953.

47. *Keepapitchinin, The* (Salt Lake City), May 1, 1870; July 4, 1871.

48. Larson, Andrew Karl. *The Red Hills of November*. Salt Lake City: Deseret News Press, 1957.

49. *Latter-day Saints Hymnal*. Salt Lake City: Deseret News Press, 1871.

50. *Latter-day Saints Psalmody*. Salt Lake City: Deseret News Press, 1889.

51. Laws, G. Malcolm, Jr. *American Balladry from British Broadsides*. Philadelphia: The American Folklore Society, 1964.

52. ———. *Native American Folksong*. Philadelphia: The American Folksong Society, 1964.

53. Lomax, John A. *Cowboy Songs and Other Frontier Ballads*. New York: Sturgis and Walton Company, 1910.

54. ———, and Alan Lomax. *Cowboy Songs and Other Frontier Ballads*. New York: Macmillan, 1938.

55. Lyon, David R. *Songs of a Pioneer*. Salt Lake City: Magazine Printing Co., 1923.

56. *Millennial Star* (London, England), 1840–1860. Official organ of the Church of Jesus Christ of Latter-day Saints in Great Britain.

57. Put. *Golden Songster*. San Francisco: D. E. Appleton Co., 1858.

58. ———. *Golden West Songster*. San Francisco: D. E. Appleton Co., 1857.

59. ———. *Original California Songster*. San Francisco: D. E. Appleton Co., 1868.

60. Randolph, Vance. *Ozark Folksongs*. 4 vols. Columbia: Historical Society of Missouri, 1946.

61. Sandburg, Carl. *The American Songbag*. New York: Harcourt, Brace, 1927.

62. Snow, Eliza R. *Poems: Religious, Historical and Political*. Vol. I, Liverpool: F. D. Richards, 1856; Vol. II, Salt Lake City: L.D.S. Printing and Publishing Establishment, 1877.

63. Swan, Howard. "The Music of the Mormons, 1830–1865," *The Huntington Library Quarterly*, XII, No. 3 (May 1949), 223–252.

64. ———. *Music in the Southwest, 1825 to 1950*. San Marino, California: Huntington Library, 1952.

65. Toelken, J. Barre. "The Ballad of the Mountain Meadows Massacre," *Western Folklore*, XVIII, No. 2 (April 1959), 169–172.

66. Willes, William. *The Mountain Warbler*. Salt Lake City: The Deseret News Book and Job Establishment, 1872.

Recordings

67. Emrich, Duncan. *Songs of the Mormons and Songs of the West*. Library of Congress, AAFS L30.

68. Fife, Austin E., and Alta S. Fife. Fife Mormon Collection. Most of this collection is in the Library of Congress.

69. Goddard, Lieberson. *The Mormon Pioneers*. Thomas E. Cheney, Consultant. Legacy Collection Album, Columbia Record LL1023, 1965.

70. Hilton, L. M. *Mormon Songs*. Folkways Record FA 2036 (FP36), 1952.

71. Sorrels, Rosalie. *Songs of the Mormon Pioneers*. Edited by Austin E. Fife. Columbia Research Group, Salt Lake City, 1964.

INDEX OF TITLES AND FIRST LINES OF SONGS

A church without a prophet is not the church for me: 144
"All Are Talking of Utah": 108–109
"All Hail the Brave Battalion": 40
All hail the brave battalion, this noble valiant band: 40
Altho' in woods and tents we dwell: 49
At the head of great Echo, there's a railroad begun: 95

"Be Home Early Tonight, My Dear Boy": 150–152; music, 151
"Bless Brigham Young": 98; music, 98
"Bless Brigham Young," we children pray: 98
"Blue Mountain": 135–137; music, 136
"Brigham, Brigham Young": 176–178; music, 177
"Brigham's Hard Times Come Again No More": 91–92
"Brigham Young, the Western Pioneer": 69–71; music, 70
"Brigham Young's Birthday": 99
"Brighter Days in Store" ("Brigham's Hard Times Come Again No More"): 91–92
Bright lights were shining in the hall: 198
"Bullfight on the San Pedro, The": 42–45; music, 43
"Bull Whacker, The": 61–63; music, 62
"Burlesque on the Fashions of the Day, 1870, A" ("The Grecian Bend"): 154–156; music, 155

"California": 57–59
"Campaign for General Smith": 33–35
"Campfire Meeting, The" ("Gather Round the Campfire, Brethren"): 75–76; music, 75
"Camp of Israel, The": 49–50
"Carrot Greens": 145–156
"Charlie Knell's Wedding": 160–161; music, 160
"Christine LeRoy": 189–190; music, 190
"Church without a Prophet, A": 144–145
"Cold Winter Is Coming": 164–165; music, 165
Cold winter is coming, there's frost in the air: 164
Come all my good people and listen to my song: 32
Come all ye feeling faithful Saints who've crossed the prairie drear: 60
Come all ye gents and ladies: 154
Come all ye people if you want to hear: 70
Come all you sons of liberty: 203

Come brethren listen to my song: 84
Come, brudder sailors, and don't you fall asleep: 172
Come, girls, come and listen to my noise: 186
Come, then, O Americans rally to the standard of liberty: 35
"Conference Time": 110

Dear friends, I pray just lend an ear: 105
"Desert Route, The": 41–42
"Ditches Break Again No More": 153–154
"Don't Marry the Mormon Boys": 186–188; music, 187
"Doo Dah": 84–86; music, 85
"Double Tragedy, The": 197–200
"Down in Utah": 130–132; music, 131
"Drunkards of Bonanza, The": 120–122
"Dying Prophet, The": 99–101

"Echo Canyon": 94–96; music, 95
"Ever Constant": 83

Forty years ago and over God's command was given: 91

"Gather Round the Campfire, Brethren": 75–76; music, 75
Gather round the campfire, brethren: 75
God bless the chosen Seer: 99
"Good Old Keg of Wine, The": 152–153
"Good Old Yankee Doodle, The": 184–185
"Gospel News Is Sounding, The": 103–105
"Grecian Bend, The": 154–156; music, 155
Greetings to thee, Sego Lily: 74

"Handcart Song, The": 64–66; music, 65
"Handcart Song, The" (Missionary): 66–67
"Have Courage, My Boy, To Say No!": 148–150; music, 149
"Have you heard of Porter Rockwell?": 191
How many old-timers remember the day: 110

I came to this land with a gun in my hand: 139
"If Uncle Sam's Determined": 86–87
If Uncle Sam's determined: 87
In ancient days they came to pass: 121
In a shaky wagon we ride: 54
"In Defense of Polygamy": 80–81; music, 81
In forty-six we bade adieu: 47
In Kanab they will always remember: 193
Into the West when dawned: 52
"Iron Horse, The": 97–98
"Is the Story True?": 78–79; music, 79
I saw Adam leave that garden with an apple in his hand: 111
I've traveled through life and I've seen many things: 150
I will sing of the Mormons, the people of the Lord: 92

"Johnston's Army Episode": 87–89
"Joseph, Joseph, Joseph, Joseph"; softly murmured Zion's chief: 100
"Julius Hannig's Wedding": 158–159; music, 159

"Kanab Tragedy, The": 193–195
Kinderhoos, Kass, Kalhoun, or Klay: 35

"Lifeboat, The": 172–173; music, 173
"Loafer's Lament, The": 161–162
"Lo a Temple": 123–124; music, 124
Lo a temple long expected in St. George shall stand: 123
"Logan Temple": 126–128; music, 127
"Lonesome Roving Wolves, The": 46

"Marching to Dixie": 116–117
"Marriage Proposal, A": 182
Mary Steavens she had disappeared: 195
"Merry Mormons, The": 187–188
"Mogos, Nogos, Everybody Come": 166–168; music, 167
"Mormon Battalion Song": 35–40; music, 38
"Mormon Battalion Song, The": 47–48
"Mormon Coon, The": 183–184
"Mormon Sunday School Song, The": 168–169
"Mormon Tabernacle, The": 101–103; music, 102
"Mottos on the Wall": 170–172; music, 171
"Mountain Meadows Massacre": 200–205; music, 203
My home it was in Texas: 136
"My House": 132; music, 132
My house is built by an old sheep corral: 132

No, brother, 'twill never be better: 189
"None Can Preach the Gospel like the Mormons Do": 142–144; music, 143
No purse, no script, they bear with them, but cheerfully they start: 67
Now I pray you be still and I'll hush your noise: 125
Now white folks, your attention, and I'll sing to you a song: 158
Now you co-habs still dodging 'round, you better keep on underground: 82

Oh, don't you remember sweet Betsy from Pike: 184
Oh, how well do I remember, when thoughts of bygone days—: 153
Oh, I'm a jolly driver on the Salt Lake City line: 62
Oh, once I lived in Cottonwood and owned a little farm: 118
Oh, Timpanogas, mighty Timpanogas: 138
Oh, touch not the wine cup, dear brother, I pray: 146
Oh, what a desert place was this: 114
Old Brigham Young was a Mormon bold: 176
Old Port Rockwell has work to do: 192
Old Zack he came to Utah: 179

"Once I Lived in Cottonwood": 118–120; music, 119
On Zion's land there shall be rest: 58
"Orderville Murder, The": 195–197
"Our Ain Mountain Hame": 59–60
"Ox Team Trail, The": 51–54; music, 52

"Passing Through": 111–112; music, 111
"Pioneer Day 1870": 105–108; music, 106
"Pleasant Valley": 133–135; music, 134
"Porter Rockwell": 191
"Pounding Rock into the Temple Foundation": 125
"Put You into Limbo": 82

"Railroad Cars, They're Coming, The": 96–97

"St. George and the Drag-on": 113–115; music, 115
"St. George and Mormon Dixie": 117–118
St. George is bright and sunny: 117
Say, Susan, wilt thou come with me: 182
Seagull, gentle Seagull: 78
"Seagulls and the Crickets, The": 76–78; music, 77
"Sego Lily": 73–74; music, 74
Sitting in a corner, on a Sunday eve: 157
Some six or seven years ago this country looked forlorn: 116
"Song for the Temple Volunteers": 126
"Sparking Sunday Night": 156–158; music, 157
"Story of Mormonism, The": 26–31; music, 27
"Strong Is the Power of Brigham's God": 89–90
Strong is the power of Brigham's God: 89
"Sweet Betsy from Pike": 184–185

"Teton Peaks": 138–140; music, 139
The battalion encamped, by the side of the grove: 46
The dear ones now have all been scattered: 83
The Gospel news is sounding to nations far and near: 103
The great Pacific Railway: 96
The Iron Horse draweth nigh: 93
The Iron Horse is coming here: 97
The Lord made Satan and Satan made sin: 166
The other night I had a dream: 145
The Prophet Nephi was brave and strong: 168
There is a bunch of whiskey bloats perluding our fair land: 80
There's a land far away in the west: 61
There's a mound in the midst of our city: 127
There's a time in each year when the boys do feel queer: 152
There's a wealth of pure affection: 170
The Saints a tabernacle reared: 101
The Upper California—Oh, that's the land for me: 68
The winter of forty-nine had passed: 77

"Thirty Pieces of Silver": 169–170
"This Is the Place": 72–73
"This Is the Place" ("Brigham Young, the Western Pioneer"): 69–71; music, 70
"This is the place for the Temple Square": 72
"Timpanogas, Mighty Timpanogas, Oh": 137–138; music, 137
'Tis a sad but true story, from the Bible it came: 169
'Tis the last greenback dollar left crumpled alone: 161
"Tittery-Irie-Aye": 31–33; music, 32
"Touch Not the Wine Cup, Oh": 146–148; music, 147
'Twas in the month of April when our youngest widow wed: 160

Under the command of Colonel Cook: 43
"United Order, The": 90–91; music, 90
"Upper California, The": 68–69; music, 68
"Utah Iron Horse, The": 92–94; music, 94

"Waste Not, Want Not": 162–164; music, 163
"Way We Crossed the Plains, The": 54–55; music, 55
We're going to preach the Gospel: 142
"We the Boys of Sanpete County": 128–129
We the boys of Sanpete County, in obedience to the call: 129
We've heard fantastic tales for years: 27
What peace and joy pervade my soul: 188
"Wheat": 192
When a child I lived at Lincoln with my parents on the farm: 162
When Mormon trains were journeying through: 38
When Uncle Sam he first set out his army to destroy us: 87
When you go to Pleasant Valley: 133
While here beneath the sultry sky: 41
While the workmen stopped in Denver: 130
"Whoa, Haw, Buck and Jerry Boy": 50–51; music, 50
Who'd ever think that Utah would stir the world so much: 109
With a merry little jig and a gay little song: 51

Yankee Doodle is the tune some Yankee chap invented: 185
"Ye Elders of Israel": 55–57; music, 56
Ye Elders of Israel, come join now with me: 56
Ye Saints throughout the mountains, pray listen to my rhyme: 126
Ye saints who dwell on Europe's shore: 64
Young Abraham left home one day: 183
You've started today on life's journey: 148

"Zack, the Mormon Engineer": 179–181; music (version A), 180
Zack Black came to Utah back in Eighty-three: 181
"Zion, the Home of an Honest Man": 61

INDEX

Adams, Frank: 198
alcoholic beverages: belief in abstinence from, 16, 120, 126, 141, 146, 150; and "drinking song," 152; Porter Rockwell and, 192. *See also* wine
amalgamation: of folksongs, 26
"Annie Laurie": 117
anti-Mormon songs: sung by Mormons, 9, 174; reaction of Mormons to, 203. *See also* Mormon songs
apostles: in Church, 144
Arizona: 133, 198
Arkansas: 175, 200–202
"At the Matinee": 16

ballads: British, 18–19; Child, 169. *See also* Mormon songs; songs
"Bald Head End of the Broom": 16
baptism: Mormon beliefs concerning, 123
Bateman, William: 201
Battalion, Mormon. *See* Mormon Battalion
Beaver, Utah: 201
Big Cottonwood Canyon: 84
birth control: Mormon beliefs concerning, 13–14, 186. *See also* childbearing
Black, Zack: 179
Black's Fork: 88
"Blind Child, The": 198
"Blind Child's Prayer, The": 16
Blue Mountain: 135
Bonanza (mining town): 120–121
"Bonnie Breast Knots, The": 188
Book of Mormon: translation of, and founding of Church, 25–26; and concept of Zion, 57; "Deseret" from, 75; stories from, in song, 166. *See also* Mormon theology
"Brennan on the Moor": 12
Brigham Young University: 137

"Bright Amanda": 11
British ballads: *See* ballads
Buchanan, James: and Johnston's Army, 84
bundling: 156
bustles: 154

California: as term for western U.S., 36, 68
Carrot County: Sanpete County, Utah, as, 145
carrots: 145
"Casey Jones": 12
Carthage, Illinois: Joseph Smith in, 34
cattle, draft. *See oxen*
cattle, longhorn: fight with, 36–37
cattle raising: Mormons and, 11–12
Cedar City: 200–201
"Charles A. Guiteau": 15
"Chevy Chase": xii
Child ballads: No. 23, 169
childbearing: 186. *See also* birth control
children: games of, 82. *See also* birth control; childbearing; family life
Church, Mormon. *See* Church of Jesus Christ of Latter-day Saints
Church of Jesus Christ of Latter-day Saints: founding of, 7–8, 23–26; devotion of members of, 7–8; and folksinging, 11; services of, 14, 116, 142, 148, 166; Priesthood office of, 26 and n.; and polygamy, 80; General Conference of, 110; plans of, for self-sustaining empire, 113–114; "calls" settlers, 113–114, 116, 118; youth groups in, 166. *See also Book of Mormon*; missionaries; Mormons; Mormon theology; polygamy
Clay, Henry: and Smith Campaign, 32
coffee: as harmful, 148
comic songs. *See* humorous songs
"Corduroy": 16

"Cork leg": 125
Cottonwood (Mormon settlement): settlers called from, 118
Council Bluffs, Iowa: 36, 54
courtship: folk terms for, 156
"Cowboy's Lament, The": 12
cowboy songs: 10, 11–12
crickets: destruction of crops by, 10, 76–77
Cumorah (hill in New York): and plates of *Book of Mormon*, 25
"Curtains of Night": 16

dance: soft-shoe, 121; Texan and, 135; murder at, 197; Church and, 187; at weddings, 158
Denver and Rio Grande railroad: 179
"Derby Ram, The": 18
Deseret: meaning of, 75; as territory, 84
"Dick Turpin": 12
didacticism: and emotionalism, 15; in Mormon songs, 61, 103, 141–142, 170; and prohibition of strong drink, 148, 150; and gambling, 150; and practice of economy, 162
Dime Song Book, The: 61–62
Dixie, Utah's: as Mormon outpost, 113–114, 116; hardships in, 118; grapes raised for wine in, 120–121
Doctrine and Covenants: 146
Driggs (President of Teton Stake of Church): 138
drinking. *See* alcoholic beverages; wine
Drummond, William W.: 84
"Drunkard's Dream, The": 146
"Drunkard's Lone Child, The": 146
"Dying Cowboy, The": 11

Echo Canyon: Mormon defenses in, 87–88, 89; railroad to, 92, 94
economies: pioneer practices of, 162
"Egyptian, reformed": as language of *Book of Mormon*, 166
education: Church emphasis on, 15
emotionalism: in religion, 14–16. *See also* sentimentality; sentimental songs
"Englishman, The": 61
"Evening Star, The": 13
excommunication: of polygamists, 175

"Fair Charlotte": 15
"Fallen Leaf": 11
family life: and religion, 13–14. *See also* birth control; childbearing; marriage; polygamy
Fancher, Capt. Charles: 201
feud: over water, 193
Fillmore, Willard: and conflict with Mormons, 84
"Finnegan's Wake": 18
folk-culture, Mormon: richness of, 141–142
folksinging: and Mormon loyalty, 8; Mormon tradition of, 10. *See also* ballads; Mormon songs; songs; tunes
Ford (governor of Illinois): 34
Foster, Charles A.: 34
Foster, Robert D.: 34
Fountain Green, Utah: 164
"Frankie and Johnny": 189
freighting: to Heber valley, 133. *See also* oxen
"Froggie Went a Courtin' ": 13

gambling: 150
games, children's: 82
Gentiles: non-Mormons as, 11, 49, 187; mentioned, xi, 9, 191
"Give Him One More as He Goes": 18
"Good Old Summer Time, The": 152
government, federal. *See* government, United States
government, United States: and polygamy, 80, 82, 83, 175; Mormon animosity toward, 84; sends army to Deseret, 84, 86–88, 141, 200; and problems of statehood for Utah, 108–109
Green River (Wyoming): drownings in, 128
Guest, Edgar A.: 142

Hancock, Levi: in Mormon Battalion, 36
handcarts: used by pioneers, 10, 64; used by missionaries, 66; mentioned, 92
Harney, General William S.: 86
"Haunted Falls": 11
Heber, Utah: 113
Heber Valley: 133
hillbilly songs: 10, 17
"Home on the Range": 12
horns: folklore of, and Mormons, 28 n.
"How Firm a Foundation": 40
humorous songs: sung by Mormons, 13, 16–18; polygamy as subject of, 179

Hutchings, Shepherd P.: in Smith Campaign, 35
hymns, Mormon: love of mountains in, 4–6; mentioned, 144 n.

"I Can't Change It": 16
Idaho: pioneer hardships in, 113; songs from, 138, 150
"I Had But Fifty Cents": 16
Illinois: Mormons in, 4, 26, 33–35, 61; mentioned, 8, 86
immigrants: Mormon, from Europe, 54, 59–60, 61; and handcarts, 64. *See also* pioneers, Mormon
Indians: as subjects of songs, 11; at Mountain Meadows Massacre, 201
intellectualism: in Mormon Church, 15, 142
Iowa City, Iowa: 64
irrigation ditches: 153, mentioned, 121
Israel: as term for Mormons, 49
"I Wish I Was Single": 16

Jackson, Wyoming: 138
Jackson's Hole: 138
jealousy: and polygamy, 189
"Jesse James": 12
Johnston, Albert Sidney: 84. *See also* Johnston's Army
Johnston's Army: 8, 84, 86–88, 89, 200, 201
Juab County, Utah: pioneer life in, 113, 132
Judas Iscariot: 169
"Just Before the Battle, Mother": 129
"Just Set a Light": 12, 15
"Just Thirty-Five": 16

Kane, Col. Thomas L.: 88
"Key Hole in the Door": 17–18
Keysor, Guy: on bullfight, 37

"Lady Isabel and the Elf Knight": 19
Laramie, Wyoming: 128
"Lass of Mohea, The": 11
"Last Rose of Summer, The": 161
Law, William: 34
law: martial, in Deseret, 87–88; enforcement of, in Deseret, 191
"Lawyer Outwitted, The": 18
"Leader of the People, The": story by John Steinbeck, 11
Leany, Hyrum: and mining town songs, 120–121
Lee, John D.: 201

Logan, Utah: pioneer life in, 113; temple in, 121–127
Lyon, John: as folk poet, 60

McCord, Joe: 197–198
McNelly, Father Tom: 121
Mahonri (character from *Book of Mormon*): 166
Manifesto, the: prohibits polygamy, 111, 175
"Marching Through Georgia": 26, 109, 116, 128
Margetts, Phillip: 66
marriage: in the Church, 13–14; customs, 158, 174–176; burdens of, for wife, 186, 189; of Mormons, to non-Mormons, 187. *See also* polygamy
"Marriage of Sir Gawain, The": 19
martial law: declared in Deseret, 87–88
martyr: Joseph Smith as, 34, 35
Melchizedek Priesthood: 142
Merrill, Harrison R.: 137
Mexico: U.S. war with, 35–37
Millennial Star: and immigrants, 61
mining: Mormon settlers and, 120–121
missionaries: supervision of, 26 n.; and foreign converts, 57–58; handcarts used by, 66; attitudes of, 142; teachings of, 144; as importers of songs, 172; Parley Pratt as, 175
Missouri: Mormons in, 4, 26, 200–202
Monticello, Utah: pioneer life in, 113; Blue Mountain near, 135; murder at, 197–198
Moriancumer (character from *Book of Mormon*): 166
Mormon Battalion: 9, 35–37
"Mormon Battalion, and First Wagon Road Over the Great American Desert, The": 37
"Mormon Car, The": 97 n.
Mormons: persecution of, 4, 26, 36, 130, 200; general characteristics of, 7; loyalty of, 7–9, 33, 108–109, 187; as folksingers, 10–11; family life of, 13–14; sentimentality of, 14–15; hostility of, to enemies, 80, 200; pride of, 130; humor of, 185; and Mountain Meadows Massacre, 202; and anti-Mormon song, 203. *See also* Church of Jesus Christ of Latter-day Saints; immigrants; Mormon songs; pioneers

Mormon songs: historical accuracy of, xi, 22, 36, 42, 111, 141, 158; as folksongs, xii; popular singers of, xii-xiv; effect of pioneer life on, 7; sex taboos in, 19; supernatural in, 19; artistry of, 20; customs and teachings in, 141; didacticism in, 61, 103, 141–142, 170; humor and parody in, 166; sentimentality in, 170. *See also* ballads; folksinging; hymns, Mormon; songs; tunes

Mormon Tabernacle: building of, 101

Mormon theology: general view of, 7; and prophets, 8; on marriage and children, 13–14; in songs, 22, 172; basis of, 26; and pioneer attitudes, 62; and folk culture, 141. *See also* Church of Jesus Christ of Latter-day Saints

Moroni: appears in vision, 25

"Mountain Dew": 16

Mountain Meadows Massacre: 174, 200–202, 203

mountains: Mormons' love of, 4–6

Mount Pisgah (Mormon camp): 36

Mt. Pleasant, Utah: 128

music. *See* tunes

murder: as song subject, 18, 174; Porter Rockwell and, 191, 192; over water, 193; at Orderville, 195; at celebration, 197–198

murder organization, secret: 84

Murdock, Captain: 54

"Mustard Plaster, The,": 16

Mutual Improvement Association: 166

Nash, Isaac B.: on Johnston's Army, 84

Nauvoo, Illinois: death of Joseph Smith in, 33–35; Mormons leave, 61; mentioned, 8, 86

Nauvoo Expositor, The: 34

Nauvoo Legion: and death of Joseph Smith, 34; in Deseret, 87–88, 89

"Nay Speak No Ill": 72

Negro songs: influence of, on Mormon songs, 172, 183

New York: Mormons in, 4; Church founded in, 7–8, 23–26; World's Fair in, 144

"O'er the Lea": 103

Ohio: Mormons in, 4, 26; Smith Campaign in, 35

"Old Arm Chair, The": 18

"Old Folks, Young Folks, Everybody Come": 166, 168

"Old Knot Hole, The": 17

Orderville, Utah: United Order in, 90, 195

Oregon: as term for western U.S., 36

organ, Mormon Tabernacle: 101

outlaw songs: 10, 12–13

oxen: used by pioneers, 61–62, 64, 92

Paiute Indians: at Mountain Meadows Massacre, 201

patriarchal order: in Mormon families, 14. *See also* family life

persecution. *See* Mormons, persecution of

Pioneer Day Celebration: 197–198

pioneers: hardships of, 8–9, 113–114, 118, 162; singing of, 10–11, 68, 156; and persecution, 26; use of oxen by, 61–62, 64, 92; and naming of Deseret, 75; and seagulls and crickets, 76–77; and carrot greens, 145; and irrigation ditches, 153; home life of, mentioned, 170; "called" by Church, 197. *See also* immigrants; Mormons

plurality of wives, doctrine of. *See* polygamy

politics: Joseph Smith in, 33–35; Church and, 105

Polk, James K.: and Mormon Battalion, 35–36

polygamy: as religious belief, 7, 13–14, 80; humor of, 16, 174–176, 179, 182, 183, 185, 189; and lore of horns, 28 n.; Joseph Smith and, 34; as term for polygyny, 80 n.; federal government and, 82; arrests for practice of, 82, 83, 175; and problems of statehood, 109; prohibition of, 111, 175; history of, in Church, 174–175; excommunication for practice of, 175

polygyny. *See* polygamy

"Poor Little Joe": 15

"Poor Wayfaring Man of Grief, A": 83

Pratt, Parley P.: 3–4, 176

prophets: belief in, 8, 9; Brigham Young as, 69; President of Church as, 116; necessity of, 144

proselyting. *See* missionaries

railroad: coming of, to Utah, 92; in Echo Canyon, 94; reaction to, 93, 97; D. & R.G., 179

railroad songs: 10, 12
"Red River Valley": 12
"reformed Egyptian": as language of *Book of Mormon*, 166
revelation, divine: belief in, 8, 26; and pioneers, 9; and Joseph Smith, 25; Church founded on, 144
revenge: for persecution, 200
Richards, Franklin D.: 92–93
Rio Virgin Valley (Utah): 113–114
Roach, Tom: as murderer, 197–198
Rockwell, Porter: and Johnston's Army, 84; as folk hero, 174; account of, 191, 192
"Root Hog or Die": 61–62
"Rose that All Are Praising, The": 144 n.
Roundy, William: 193
"Row Your Boat": 15–16

sailor songs: mentioned, 172
St. George, Utah: poverty in, 113; temple-building in, 113, 121, 123, 125, 126; mentioned, 158, 200
"Saint George and the Dragon": 113
"Salem": 58
Salt Lake City: proposed burning of, 86–87; mentioned, 201
"Sam Bass": 12
Sanpete County, Utah: pioneer life in, 113, 145; mentioned, 128, 130
satire: in Mormon songs, 174–176. *See also* humorous songs
seagulls: and crickets, 10, 76–77
Seegmiller, Dan: 193
Seeley, William Stewart: 128
sego lily: 73–74
sentimental songs: sung by Mormons, 14–15; mid-Victorian, 146. *See also* sentimentality
sentimentality: in poetry, 142; and prohibition of drink, 148; in Mormon songs, 170. *See also* sentimental songs
sex: in Mormon songs, 19
Sharp, John: 93
"Ship that Never Returned, The": 15
shivaree: at pioneer wedding, 158
"Sioux Indians, The": 11
Smith, George A.: 114
Smith, Hyrum: 34
Smith, Joseph: murder of, 4, 34; as prophet, 8, 34; and other sects, 23–24; establishes Church, 23–26; vi-sions of, 24–25; presidential campaign of, 33–35; and polygamy, 80, 174, 175; as commander of Nauvoo Legion, 87–88; and Brigham Young, 99–100; and Porter Rockwell, 191
Smith, Lot: 88
smoking: prohibition of, 126
Snow, Eliza R.: as wife of Brigham Young, 37
"Solomon Levi": 191

songs: anti-Mormon, 9, 174, 203; cowboy, 10, 11–12; hillbilly, 10, 17; outlaw, 10, 12–13; railroad, 10, 12; humorous, 13, 16–18, 179; sentimental, 14–15, 146; Negro, 172, 183; sailor, 172. *See also* ballads; folksinging; hymns, Mormon; Mormon songs; tunes
Spencer, Clarissa Young: daughter of Brigham Young, 92–93
sparking: as term for courtship, 156
spooning: as term for courtship, 156
Stake President: authority of, 138
statehood: of Utah, 105, 108
Steinbeck, John: on westering, 11
Stoddard, Jud: 84
"Strawberry Roan, The": 12
Sunday School: Mormon, 166
supernatural: in Mormon songs, 19
"Sussannah, Oh": 66

"Take Me Home": 15
Taylor, John: 68
tea: as harmful, 148
temples: building of, 8, 101, 113, 121, 123, 125, 126–127; functions of, 123; nonmembers in, 126
Temple Square, Salt Lake City: 101
testimony, religious: 14, 15
Teton Basin, Idaho: life in, 113; description of, 138
Teton County, Idaho: 113
"Texas Boys": 186
"Texas Ranger, The": 11
theocratic social system: at Orderville, 90
theology, Mormon. *See* Mormon theology
Timpanogas (mountain): annual hike to, 137
tithe paying: mentioned, 126
tobacco: use of, forbidden, 148

tunes (used for songs in this collection): "Marching Through Georgia," 26, 109, 116, 126; "How Firm a Foundation," 40; "Salem," 58; "The Englishman," 61; "Nay Speak No Ill," 72; "A Poor Wayfaring Man of Grief," 83; "Hard Times Come Again No More," 91, 153; "O'er the Lea," 103; "Vilikins and His Dinah," 110; "Annie Laurie," 117; "Cork Leg," 125; "Just Before the Battle, Mother," 129; "Turnip Greens," 145; "The Good Old Summer Time," 152; "The Last Rose of Summer," 161; "Texas Boys," 186; "The Bonnie Breast Knots," 188; "Solomon Levi," 191; "The Blind Child," 198
"Turnip Greens": 145

Utah County, Utah: 113
Utah: achieves statehood, 105. *See also* Deseret
"Utah Carrol": 12
Utah Pioneer Trails and Landmarks Association: 201
United Order: defined, 90; at Orderville, 195
Urim and Thummin: and *Book of Mormon*, 25

"Valley of Custer": 11
vaudeville: 183
Verdure, Utah: 198
Victorian morality: 141–142, 146
"Vilikins and His Dinah": 110

"Wabash Cannonball, The": 12
Walton, Mrs. Jane: 197–198
Warsaw, Illinois: 34
Washington, Utah: 158
Washington County, Utah: 200

water: dispute over, 193. *See also* irrigation ditches
Weber Canyon: 93
Wells, General Daniel H.: 87, 89
"We Thank Thee, Oh God, for a Prophet": 144 n.
"wheat": as war cry, 192
"When the Work's All Done This Fall": 12
"White Man, Let Me Go": 11
"Whoa, Mule, Whoa": 18
"Whummil Bore, The": 17
wine: grapes raised for, 120–121; at Mormon wedding, 158
Winter Quarters: 76
"Woman, Naughty Woman": 16
Woodruff, Wilford: issues Manifesto, 80, 111, 175
"Word of Wisdom": 148
"Wreck of Number 9, The": 12
"Wreck of the Old 97": 12
Wyoming: 64

Young, Brigham: as prophet, 8; Johnston's Army, 8, 84, 86–88, 89; and polygamy, 13–14, 80, 174–175; and Mormon Battalion, 36; as pioneer leader, 62; as governor of Deseret, 84, 87–88; and railroad, 92–93; as subject of song, 98, 99, 184; death of, 99–100; at St. George, 114; and Green River tragedy, 128; and Porter Rockwell, 191; and Mountain Meadows Massacre, 201; mentioned, 9, 37
Young, Joseph A.: 93
Yokel, Mike: 138

"Zebra Dun": 12
Zion: Mormon concept of, 3–6, 15, 55, 57–58, 59–60, 61, 141; and Mormon folk culture, 141
"Zion's Standard": 3–4